Keto Vegan Cookbook For Beginners

Cynthia Allen

Contents

INTRODUCTION

Three years ago, I experienced a burning and sharp lower-back pain; then, as time went on, it got worse especially after prolonged sitting or standing. I was tired and bloated all the time and I've even suffered from the winter blues. I felt like an old person. Shortly after that, I started gaining weight despite regular exercise and healthy eating habits! I started a diet, lost some pounds, and then, I started gaining weight again. I did it again and I was bitterly disappointed with my results. I experienced the problem that many of us face, the so-called yo-yo effect. It is obvious that longer periods of caloric restriction can lead to physical and mental stress. I was always hungry because diets and low-calorie intake can disrupt hormones that control appetite and satiety. The fat cells in our body produce leptin, the hormone that controls hunger levels. When we go on a restrictive dietary regimen, the amount of leptin in our body can drastically drop. Consequently, it increases our appetite and our hunger; in other words, due to low levels of leptin, our body tends to refill its fat cells. To make matters worse, I was prediabetic according to my glucose levels.

Ironically, I had been cooking at home for years and was mostly eating organic and local foods. However, I got clear signs – You are on a bad diet that that doesn't fit your lifestyle and your needs; simply put, a wrong diet sets you up for failure! Sometimes we need the rude awakening because we usually learn the hard way. I realize – I can complain about these bad things that happened to me and feel miserable, or I can see these problems as a challenge. This "bad situation" might help me reach my health goals. This situation taught me an important lesson – there is no temporary and quick solution. I have to say goodbye to my old habits, I have to make my eating habits realistic and sustainable. Luckily, I discovered the vegan ketogenic diet! When following this dietary regimen, you should focus on low-carb vegan-friendly foods and avoid high-carb foods.

As you probably already know, the most disease begins in the gut. I know that a healthy lifestyle is a challenging goal, so I created this recipe collection to help you stop with perpetual dieting, lose weight and prevent some serious conditions in a healthy way; this cookbook can help you kick-start your keto journey and stay on track. In real life, sometimes you win, sometimes you lose learn, but if you make health your primary focus in life, you'll always win!

Basic Vegan Keto Diet Rules

The vegan keto diet is a low-carb, high-fat, and moderate-protein plant-based diet; in addition, this diet excludes all animal-based foods (e.g. meat, dairy products, and eggs). How does the vegan keto diet work? Our body uses carbohydrates (glucose) as its primary energy source. Hence, a low-carb diet causes our body to transform fatty acids into ketones; consequently, our body uses ketones as the primary energy source instead of glucose (carbohydrates). Simply put, to implement this diet correctly, it's important to focus on healthy foods that are high in fat and low in carbs. Your goal should be to get 70 to 75 percent of your daily calories from fat and about 20 to 25 percent from protein; you should limit your total carbohydrate consumption to 35 grams or less per day.

In essence, a ketogenic diet is the type of a diet human beings ate for thousands of years. The ketogenic diet promotes real, single-ingredient foods as a high-quality source of vitamins, minerals, and other beneficial nutrients. You can watch your portions, exercise and think positive, but if you do not eat real foods, you can't expect a real transformation. The real food is whole, unprocessed food that is rich in nutrients and free of chemical additives. Additionally, you should cook real food at home as much as possible and your body will thank you!

On the other hand, processed foods are foods that contain more than one item on the list of ingredients and they have been chemically processed. They became popular in the 20th century. While processed food such as canned goods, ready-to-eat meals, savory snacks, and packaged foods are convenient, they are also bad for our health. Processed foods are often loaded with salt, sugar, and fat that can have devastating effects on our health and well-being. Moreover, most highly processed foods usually contain artificial flavor, colorants, and preservatives. Not surprisingly, consumption of processed foods is strongly associated with some of the most serious diseases including heart disease, obesity, diabetes, cancer, and mental disorders. To sum up, buy organic and local foods whenever you can and focus on whole, plant-based foods that have grown in soil and haven't been artificially created.

What to Eat on a Vegan Ketogenic Diet?

Whether you are following a keto vegan diet, or are considering trying this dietary regimen, I created this keto food list to make your keto grocery shopping easy and manageable.

<u>Vegetables</u>: Lettuce (all types), asparagus, broccoli, mushrooms, onion, garlic, arugula, avocado, bok choy, radishes, celery, squash, kohlrabi, tomatoes, cauliflower, zucchini, eggplant, and greens (spinach, kale, Swiss chard, collard, mustard greens, and turnip). In moderation: artichokes, cucumbers, cabbage, okra, Brussels sprouts, snap peas, snow peas, green beans, and fennel.

<u>Nuts</u>: Brazil nuts, pecans peanuts, almonds, walnuts, macadamia nuts, hazelnuts, pine nuts.

<u>Seeds</u>: Hemp seeds, pumpkin seeds, chia seeds, flax seeds, sesame seeds, and sunflower seeds.

<u>Fats & Oils</u>: Coconut oil, olive oil, flaxseed oil, cocoa butter, avocado oil, and nut oil.

<u>Fruits</u>: Lemon, lime, blackberries, raspberries, cranberries, strawberries, coconut, and tomatoes.

<u>Keto-friendly drink options</u>: Coffee, tea, sparkling water, diet soda, seltzer, vegan keto smoothies and shakes, zero carb energy drinks.

Other keto-friendly foods include:

<u>Herbs and spices</u> (fresh or dried); vegan <u>bouillon cubes</u> and granules.

<u>Sauces & Condiments</u>: Mustard, tomato sauce, vinegar, and hot sauce (make sure to check labels).

<u>Canned food</u>: tomato, sauerkraut, pickles, and olives (no added sugar).

<u>Baking ingredients</u>: coconut flour, almond flour, baking powder, baking soda, vanilla extract, sugar-free chocolate, cocoa, and glucomannan powder.

<u>Nut & Seed Butters</u>: peanut butter, hazelnut butter, walnut butter, macadamia nut butter, almond butter, coconut butter, pecan butter, sesame butter (tahini), and sunflower seed butter.

<u>Vegan Protein Sources</u>: Tofu, tempeh, jackfruit, and nutritional yeast,

<u>Vegan full-fat "dairy"</u>: Coconut yogurt, vegan butter, plant-based cheese, dairy-free milk (unsweetened).

Coconut products: Full-fat coconut milk and coconut cream.

Keto-Friendly Alcohol: Whiskey, brandy, dry martini, vodka, and tequila.

Seaweed: Wakame, spirulina, dulse, spirulina, chlorella, nori, and kelp.

Keto sweeteners: Monk fruit is a zero-carb sweetener; Splenda (sucralose-based sweetener) has 0.5g of carbs per packet (1 g); Erythritol has 4 grams of carbs per teaspoon (4 grams); Xylitol has 4 grams of carbs per teaspoon (4 grams); Stevia is a zero-carb sweetener, too.

Other Vegan Keto Favorites: Shirataki noodles, roasted seaweed, kelp noodles, kelp flakes, and nori sheets.

Foods to Avoid on a Vegan Ketogenic Diet

Grains & grain-like seeds: Rice, oats, wheat, corn, quinoa, amaranth, barley, buckwheat, corn, millet.

Legumes: Beans, lentils, and dried peas.

Starches: Starchy vegetables (potatoes, sweet potatoes, yams, parsnip, and taro), banana, sago, tapioca, plantain, and mesquite.

Flours: Wheat flour, cornmeal, arrowroot, cassava, and dal.

Sugars and Syrups: Molasses, honey, maple syrup, granulated sugar (white and brown), corn syrup, carob syrup, agave nectar, treacle, malt, rapadura, rice syrup, malt syrup, sorghum syrup, barley malt, cane juice, cane juice crystals, muscovado sugar, powdered sugar, panocha, and scant.

Fruits (other than berries) & dried fruits

Sugary drinks: soda and energy drinks.

Processed vegetable oils & trans fats: Vegetable shortening, margarine, corn oil, cottonseed oil, grapeseed oil, safflower oil, and soybean oil.

I can't stress this enough – avoid margarine at all costs! Margarine is an industrially produced imitation of butter. There are numerous reasons to avoid margarine. It is made up of polyunsaturated fats (damaging vegetable oils). Further, margarine can contain large amounts of trans fats that are extremely damaging to your health. To make things even worse, margarine products are treated with many chemicals and preservatives. For all the above reasons, margarine products might be linked to allergies, inflammatory diseases, and asthma.

From Keto to Vegan Keto:
My Favorite Vegan Substitutes

You can create delicious vegan versions of all your old favorites, trust me. This handy recipe collection will prove to you that there's a whole load of vegan solutions when it comes to replacing eggs and dairy. When it comes to buying keto-friendly products, make sure to check labels and ingredients lists.

Protein sources. On a regular keto diet, meat is one of the most important protein sources. However, with a little creativity and good meal planning, going on a vegan ketogenic plan is possible. You should consume high-quality plant-based protein sources such as low-carb soy products (tofu and tempeh), nuts, seeds, sprouted seeds, pea protein, hemp protein, and so forth.
If you are searching for vegan dairy and egg replacements, here are some suggestions and tricks.

Yogurt substitutes. Instead of yogurt and sour cream, use plant-based yogurt; you will probably be able to find some vegan options at your local food market; on the other hand, you can make plant-based yogurt at home. It is easier than you ever thought! You can use almost any non-dairy milk to make a yogurt (cashew and coconut are most popular due to large amounts of natural fats); then, it is important to choose the right yogurt starter (starter culture or probiotics); now, you can use a thickener if you prefer a spoon-able, thick yogurt but this is completely optional (agar agar and tapioca starch are good choices or you can strain your yogurt through cheesecloth); finally, you can add flavors such as vanilla and cocoa powder or your favorite sweetener. As you probably already know, your yogurt needs to ferment. Allow it to sit in a warm place for 24 to 48 hours. It can also ferment in a dehydrator for several hours. When your yogurt is done, transfer it to the refrigerator. You can make sour cream in the same way, just make sure to add less water to achieve your desired consistency.

Cheese substitutes. There are many dairy-free cheese substitutes on the market. However, you can easily make your own cheese at home. Use nuts and seeds such as almonds, cashews or sunflower to make vegan cheeses that will change your life forever! It can take a little time and effort but a homemade plant-based cheese will take your keto diet to the next level; it is definitely worth it. For a true gourmand experience, add some aromatics and herbs to improve flavor and satisfy your taste buds.

Butter substitutes. You can replace butter with coconut oil or soy butter. Make sure to avoid hydrogenated oils and use more natural fats such as avocado and nut butter. Nut butter is indeed low carb food that can help you reduce appetite and lose weight naturally; they contain good fats that reduce the risk of heart disease and diabetes. Nuts and seeds contain beneficial vitamins and minerals. For instance, walnuts are high in omega-3s, almonds are rich in calcium, cashews are loaded with iron and magnesium. Unlike expensive nuts such as cashew nuts or almonds, peanuts are a low-cost option with similar health benefits. Two tablespoons of natural peanut butter (only peanuts and salt) contain 6-7 grams of carbohydrates. You can easily make great peanut butter by using your blender or a food processor. A sunflower seed butter is also an affordable and delicious option on a vegan keto diet; it is an excellent source of vitamin E, copper, and selenium. A few recipes in this collection call for sesame butter (tahini), which is a good source of vitamin B6, iron, and zinc. Due to its versatility, you can use it in both, sweet and savory recipes.

Heavy cream substitutes. As for heavy cream, a coconut cream makes a good dairy replacement. Then, you can try mixing soy milk and olive oil (1 cup of heavy cream = 2/3 cup of soy milk + 1/3 cup of olive oil). You can also blend silken tofu with a small amount of soy milk until the mixture reaches a smooth consistency. If you need a heavy cream for rich soups and creamy sauces but you do not like coconut flavor, you can use cashews or sunflower seeds. Soak them in water overnight and process with water to make a cream-like consistency. Replace a whipped cream with a full-fat canned coconut milk that is perfect ingredient for vegan keto desserts.

Egg Substitutes. There are plenty of vegan egg substitutes so you don't have to give up on your favorites. There are companies that make vegan alternatives of everything, including ready-made vegan egg replacements! Silken tofu has a wonderfully soft texture so you can use it in many recipes such as brownies, cakes, baked goods, and many other recipes. For baking goods, feel free to experiment and get creative with blending keto vegetables and nuts into a purée.

A flax egg is a real game-changer. Simply ground flax seeds into a whole flax meal with a coffee grinder; combine one tablespoon of flax meal and three tablespoons of water; allow the mixture to set approximately 10 minutes. A flax egg will add moisture to your muffins, cookies, and pancakes, just as a regular egg would. It works incredibly well in vegan keto desserts! If you want a more neutral flavor, you can use chia seeds as a great alternative – this is the perfect natural vegan egg substitute. There is one more, simple and inexpensive option for baked goods – mix one teaspoon of baking soda with one tablespoon of white vinegar. One other thing worth mentioning is over-ripe mashed avocado; it makes a great egg substitute for brownies. When it comes to the vegan keto brownies, you can also use an apple sauce (unsweetened), vegan protein powder mixed with water, or Greek-style yogurt as egg replacers.

A Balanced Vegan Keto Diet: 6 Nutrients to Watch

Whether you are following a vegan keto diet, or are considering this eating plan, there are key nutrients to keep in mind.

Calcium is necessary for your healthy, strong bones and teeth. Aim to consume 525 mg of calcium per day at the least. You can eat mustard greens, turnip greens, broccoli, Bok choy, kale, tofu, fortified plant milk, and juices.

Iron is needed to produce red blood cells and regulate proper immune function. Aim to eat more iron-rich foods, such as nuts, seeds, and cruciferous vegetables. Iron-fortified foods, such as plant milk, can help too.

Iodine is vital for thyroid health; it plays an important role in the human body. The symptoms of its deficiency include fatigue, constipation, dry skin, weight gain, and depression. Seaweed and iodized salt are good sources of iodine as well.

Vitamin B12 is present in mushrooms grown in B12-rich soils, nutritional yeast, spirulina, chlorella, nori, and unwashed organic products.

Vitamin D is present in fortified vegan milk, fortified soy products, and mushrooms such as portobello, button, shiitake, and morel. The Sun is the number one source of vitamin D – it takes 5 to 30 minutes of sun twice per week. The symptoms of its deficiency include fatigue, depression, and muscle weakness.

Long-chain omega-3 and omega-6 fatty acids are necessary for your mental and physical health. You should eat walnuts, canola oil, sunflower oil, flaxseed oil, hemp seeds, soybean, seaweed, algae, and Brussels sprouts. If your keto vegan diet doesn't meet all the daily nutrient requirements, consider taking dietary supplements.

A related point to consider is good keto hydration. Your body needs proper hydration to optimize the creation of energy from food. Even mild dehydration can affect your energy level, memory, and cognitive function. Opt for plain water whenever you can. Drinking tea, sparkling water, and coffee is also good for keeping your body hydrated. A solid hydration plan also includes "juicy" vegetables like cucumbers, tomato, celery, radish, zucchini, and other water-rich vegetables. For instance, 94 percent of tomato's weight is water.

It is important to maintain a good fluid balance so pay attention to electrolytes (e.g. sodium, chloride, bicarbonate, potassium, phosphate, calcium, and magnesium). Consume bouillon and broth, and add salt to your food. You can also use electrolyte tablets and lite salt (a blend of regular table salt i.e. sodium chloride and potassium chloride). Mineral water is a great solution as well.

5 Science-Based Health Benefits of Eating Keto Vegan

The vegan ketogenic diet is beginning to get recognition for amazing healing benefits it can offer. Not only do you enjoy amazingly fresh and delicious foods, but you also improve your health, lose several pounds, maintain your ideal weight, and reduce the risk of many diseases. As a matter of fact, scientists have shown that a low-carb, high-fat diet has the potential to lower inflammation, stabilize blood sugar and reduce oxidative stress more effectively than any other popular diet. Although the vegan ketogenic diet does not work like a magic wand, it can inspire you and motivate you for long-term changes in your diet.

Reduced insulin levels. Eating fewer carbs and plant-based foods has a direct result in lowering blood sugar and insulin levels.

Blood pressure tends to drop significantly. Vegan keto diets are an effective way to combat high blood pressure in a natural way. Lowering your carb intake can reduce the risk of heart disease and stroke.

Reduced risk of certain cancers. The whole plant, nutrient-rich foods may benefit your health by significantly reducing the risk factors that contribute to breast, prostate, and colon cancers. Vegans generally eat vegetables, leafy greens, soy products, and nuts regularly, while limiting the consumption of processed, smoked and overcooked animal products; it may provide some protection against malignant diseases. Studies have proven that a plant-based diet may decrease your risk of dying from cancer by up to 15%.

Neuroprotective benefits. The vegan keto diet may protect your brain and mental health. It can prevent conditions like Alzheimer's, Parkinson's, dementia, and insomnia. Clinical trials have proven that this diet can cure epilepsy and improve the cognitive functioning in children.

Weight loss. In an ideal world, if someone wants to lose weight, they should burn more calories than they consume. Easier said than done! In real life, there are more than one reasons for putting on weight – genetic predisposition, aging, an underactive thyroid (hypothyroidism), hormone imbalance, hormonal changes of menopause, food addiction, high insulin levels, stress, neurologic problems, and so forth. According to statistics, nearly one-third of the population suffers from obesity. However, it's important to weigh the risks so you should consult a doctor before starting any sort of diet.

The vegan keto diet positively impacts weight and satiety since it forces your body to burn fat (not glucose) for energy. In fact, your body converts fat into ketones, which is an alternative source of energy. It also makes your cells get rid of stored carbohydrates. This process puts your body into weight loss mode. Many studies have shown that significant decrease in carb intake can result in weight loss, at least in the short term. Eating more lean protein can help too. Further, ketones suppress appetite by controlling hormones, including ghrelin aka "hunger hormone". Removing sugars and starches from your diet will force your kidneys to shed excess sodium and water out of the body, reducing bloating and water retention. In addition, plenty of protein can help reduce your appetite, build muscles, and boost your metabolism. Low carb vegetables are high in dietary fiber, which can slow the absorption of sugar and help food pass through the digestive system easily. It means that your main meals should include a protein source, a fat source, and low-carb vegetables. Keto-friendly foods not only keep you satisfied longer, but they also prevent your cells from absorbing some of the calories because they bind with fat and sugar molecules in your body.

In a nutshell, if you want to lose weight, then it can be helpful to follow a simple nutrition plan that is based on real foods. Here are the 12 steps you should follow in order to lose weight on a vegan keto diet.

1. Make sure to eat mostly natural, single-ingredient foods. Real foods such as seeds, nuts, and low-carb vegetables may boost satiety by controlling hormones that keep you feeling full. Refined and processed food, on the other hand, are satiety killers.

2. Load your plate with low-carb vegetables. Needless to say, dietary fiber is essential for a healthy diet; it is super-filling but low in calories. Some types of soluble fiber that are found in asparagus, leeks, and cabbage have been shown to increase the absorption of minerals in the foods you eat.

3. Here is another satiety secret – eat protein! Lean protein can raise levels of peptides in your stomach; peptides send out satiety signals to your brain. In addition, protein-rich foods can boost your metabolism by 80 to 100 calories per day.

4. There is a great way to trick your stomach into feeling full – drink a glass of water prior to each meal. Eight glasses of water per day is a typical guideline. On a low-carb diet, you will probably need more water. Pro tip: drink until your urine is light yellow.

5. Eat slowly and savor the flavors.

6. Do not skip breakfast. Your body needs a kick start in the morning so make sure to eat a protein-rich breakfast.

7. Mindful eating can help you control your portions. Distracted eating can lead to overeating. Numerous researchers found that those who are distracted by TV or a computer while they eat their meal are more likely to snack later on than those who focus on their meal. You should pay attention to your meal and listen to your body's signs of fullness. Do not serve meals in front of the TV and stop using your smartphone while eating. There's an additional aspect of this: eating is an important act of socialization so dining together as a family has many health benefits; it can significantly lower the likelihood of developing eating disorders too.

8. Hidden carbs are your "enemy number one." Foods that may have hidden carbs include dairy products, sauces, snack foods, condiments, salad dressing, sodas, and so forth; they can ruin your diet. If you tend to order your keto meal with extra ketchup or a few extra tablespoons of coleslaw, think twice. They can be real carb bombs! And remember, the best way to know what you're consuming is by choosing real foods and cooking at home as much as you can.

9. Stop emotional eating. People often use food to comfort themselves in difficult times; it can sabotage their weight-loss efforts. Avoid eating when feeling stressed and powerless. Close your eyes, take a deep breath and try to connect with your emotions. Ask yourself, "Am I really hungry? What do I really need at this moment?" Listen to your emotion, they are trying to communicate with you.

10. Intermittent Fasting. In essence, fasting can help you improve health, lose weight, and live longer. It can also help your body get into ketosis faster. There are multiple ways to practice intermittent fasting so you can choose the one that suits you best.

11. Cutting calorie intake by 20–30%. Generally speaking, when you consume fewer calories than needed, your body will release its fat stores and consequently you will lose pounds. Do calories matter on a vegan keto dietary regimen?

    Calories do really matter but each macronutrient (proteins, fats or carbohydrates) provides a specific number of calories. Carbs provide 4 calories per gram, Protein – 4 calories per gram, Fat – 9 calories per gram. Digestible fiber provides 2 calories per gram. Eating too many calories can lower the effect of a low-carb diet; eating fewer calories, on the other hand, can cause other health problems. Skinny but unhealthy? No thanks! Therefore, you should focus on highly-satiating low-carb foods, while cutting out all processed and highly-palatable foods. Calorie restriction can lead to longevity and better weight management as well.

12. 12. Install a Keto diet app. You can speed up your weight loss by tracking what you eat and drink so keep a food diary or install a food tracking app on your phone. These apps can help you stay motivated and save your time. They will give you a real picture of what you're eating during the day. It is very eye-opening for many dieters. You can find calorie counters, nutrient trackers, you can even find trackers for body fat, energy, and glucose levels. You can create your own shopping lists, too.

A Word about Our Recipe Collection

If you are looking for vegan keto recipes that your family won't be able to resist, this collection is worth a try. Every recipe in this collection includes the ingredients list, estimate cook time, and step-by-step instructions, and detailed nutritional analyses of macronutrients, sugar, and fiber. If you are new to the vegan keto diet, simply start with familiar and foolproof recipes like a vegetable soup or mushroom stew. You can transform any regular keto meal into a veg-friendly wonder! You've already learned some special tricks to substituting for protein, dairy and eggs. When transforming favorite desserts, always have basic ingredients on hand: cocoa powder, baking soda, coconut oil, sugar-free chocolate, nuts and seeds. White sugar isn't keto friendly? No problem! Instead, I stocked my pantry with stevia and other keto-friendly sweeteners. As for vegan baking, it is a breeze with good pantry basics: coconut milk, almond meal, apple cider vinegar, ground flax seeds, and so on. Well, it doesn't take a rocket scientist to understand the vegan keto diet!

I've been collecting recipes for at least 10 years. These recipes come from home cooks – my great-grandmother, my grandma, my two aunts, my mom, and my dear neighbor. This cookbook covers both classic and trendy recipes. You will explore the best plant-based, keto recipes, from timeless grandma's recipes and old-fashioned treats to innovative delicacies. I wish you luck on your vegan keto journey!

3-Week Meal Plan

This is a sample menu for three weeks on a vegan ketogenic diet.

DAY 1

Breakfast – Chia Chocolate Smoothie

Lunch – Japanese-Style Soup with Greens; Spicy Tofu with Peppers

Snack – Crispy Tomato Chips

Dinner – Taco Salad Boats; 1 medium tomato

DAY 2

Breakfast –Gooey Pumpkin Muffins; 1 shake of 1/2 cup of coconut milk and protein powder

Lunch – Mom's Cabbage Stew; 1 serving of cauliflower rice

Dessert – Perfect Peppermint Fudge

Dinner – Greek-Style Salad

DAY 3

Breakfast – Butternut Squash and Cocoa Bowl; 5-6 almonds

Snack – No Bake Fat Bombs

Lunch – Thick Zucchini Soup; Cauliflower Salad with Pecans

Dinner – Easy Fried Tofu with Pecans; 1 keto dinner roll; 1 cup raw baby spinach with apple cider vinegar

DAY 4

Breakfast – Southwest-Inspired Tofu Scramble; 1/2 tomato with sea salt

Lunch – Classic Mushroom Stroganoff; 1 serving of coleslaw

Dinner – Curried Oven-Roasted Cauliflower

Dessert – Chocolate Almond Cookies

DAY 5

Breakfast – The Ultimate Homemade Sandwich Rolls; 2 tablespoons sesame paste (tahini)

Lunch – Hungarian-Style Chanterelle Stew; 1 handful of mixed green salad with a few drizzles of a freshly squeezed lemon juice

Dinner – Veggie Noodles with Hot Avocado Sauce; 1 ounce vegan cheese; 1 teaspoon of mustard

DAY 6

Breakfast – Banana and Berry Milkshake; 1 keto roll
Lunch – Asparagus with Lebanese Baba Ghanoush; 1 serving of fried cauliflower rice
Snack – Tofu-Kale Dip with Crudités
Dinner – Cauliflower Rice Stuffed Peppers; 1 cucumber; 1 ounce vegan cheese

DAY 7

Breakfast – American-Style Chocolate Pancakes
Lunch – Silky Broccoli Soup; 1 large tomato; 1 cup of fried mushrooms with 1 tablespoon of olive oil
Dessert – Old-Fashioned Walnut Cookies
Dinner – Colorful Roasted Vegetables with Herbs

DAY 8

Breakfast – Multi Nut and Seed Granola; 1/2 cup of coconut yogurt
Snack – Avocado Stuffed with Tomato and Mushrooms
Lunch – Persian Stew (Khoresht Badam); 1 serving of cauliflower rice
Dinner – Guilt-Free Parmesan Zoodles

DAY 9

Breakfast – Home-Style Hazelnut "Cereal"; 1/2 cup unsweetened almond milk
Lunch – BBQ Asian Tofu with Tomato Sauce; 1 serving of cabbage salad
Dessert – Cinnamon Brownie Bars
Dinner – Parmesan-Crusted Vegetable Casserole

DAY 10

Breakfast – Chia, Blackberry and Cocoa Smoothie; 1 keto dinner roll with 1 tablespoon of peanut butter
Snack – Italian-Style Stuffed Mushrooms
Lunch – Saucy Tempeh with Brussels Sprouts; 1 scallion
Dinner – One-Skillet Tofu and Baby Artichokes; 2 tablespoons tomato paste

DAY 11

Breakfast – Autumn Chia Pudding; 1 tablespoon of peanut butter; 1 keto roll
Lunch – Simple Cauliflower Soup; Stuffed Zucchini with Tofu and Cashews
Dessert – Blackberry Jam Sandwich Cookies
Dinner – Saucy Fennel with Herb Tomato Sauce

DAY 12

Breakfast – The Ultimate Homemade Sandwich Rolls; 1 tablespoon of peanut butter; 1 table-spoon of Easy Raspberry Jam
Lunch – Mediterranean Eggplant Soup; 1 serving of low-carb grilled vegetables
Dinner – Curried Oven-Roasted Cauliflower; 1 ounce of vegan cheese

DAY 13

Breakfast – Hemp Heart Porridge with Strawberries; 1/2 cup unsweetened almond milk
Snack – Garlicky Spinach Chips with Avocado Dip
Lunch – Broccoli Aloo Masala; 1 serving of roasted keto veggies; 1 medium cucumber
Dinner – Sriracha Tofu with Greek Tzatziki Sauce

DAY 14

Breakfast – Gooey Pumpkin Muffins; 1/2 cup coconut milk (preferably homemade)
Lunch – Favorite Roasted Cabbage; 1 handful of baby spinach with 1 teaspoon of mustard and 1 teaspoon of olive oil
Dessert – Raspberry and Almond Swirl Cheesecake
Dinner – Saucy Tempeh with Brussels Sprouts

DAY 15

Breakfast – Autumn Chia Pudding
Lunch – Classic Mushroom Stroganoff; 1 serving of cauliflower rice
Dessert – Home-Style Chocolate Bar
Dinner – Cucumber and Zucchini Ribbon Salad; 1 keto roll

DAY 16

Breakfast – 1-Minute Muffin in a Mug; 1/2 cup of coconut yogurt
Snack – Authentic Mexican Guacamole; 1/2 cup raw keto vegetable sticks
Lunch – Spicy Mushroom and Broccoli Melange; Crunchy Broccoli Salad
Dinner – Moroccan Carrot Salad with Harissa; Chewy Chocolate and Peanut Butter Bars

DAY 17

Breakfast – Keto Breakfast Crunch; 2 tablespoons mixed berries (fresh or frozen)
Snack – Stuffed Avocado Boats
Lunch – Nana's Cream of Cauliflower Soup; Warm Savoy Cabbage Slaw
Dinner – Kale Salad with Crispy Tofu Cubes

DAY 18

Breakfast – Raspberry Peanut Butter Shake; 1 keto roll
Snack – Stuffed Mushrooms with Walnuts
Lunch – Japanese-Style Soup with Greens; Warm Savoy Cabbage Slaw
Dinner – Taco Salad Boats; Festive Butterscotch Blondies

DAY 19

Breakfast – The Best Avocado Cupcakes Ever
Lunch – Veggie Noodles with Hot Avocado Sauce; 1 serving of steamed broccoli
Dessert – Coconut Carrot Cake Squares
Dinner – 1 serving of grilled tofu; 1 serving of Iceberg lettuce; 1 teaspoon Dijon mustard

DAY 20

Breakfast – Chocolate Avocado Pudding
Lunch – Classic Mushroom Stroganoff; 1 serving of fried broccoli
Dinner – 1 serving of grilled tempeh; 1 medium tomato with 2-3 Kalamata olives

DAY 21

Breakfast – Tofu scramble with scallions; 1 bell pepper
Lunch – Simple Cauliflower Soup; 1 serving of roasted asparagus
Dinner – 1 serving of Shirataki noodles; 1 avocado (mashed); 2 tablespoons tomato paste

BREAKFAST

2 Servings   10 minutes

1. Chia Chocolate Smoothie

Ingredients

- 8 walnuts
- 3/4 cup almond milk
- 1/4 cup water
- 1 ½ cups lettuce
- 2 teaspoons vegan protein powder, zero carbs
- 1 tablespoon chia seeds
- 1 tablespoon unsweetened cocoa powder
- 4 fresh dates, pitted

Nutritional Information

335 Calories;
31.7g Fat;
5.7g Carbs;
7g Protein;
2.7g Fiber

Directions

Process all ingredients in your blender until everything is uniform and creamy.

Divide between two glasses and serve well-chilled.

2. Banana and Berry Milkshake

4 Servings **5 minutes**

Ingredients

- 1/2 cup water
- 1 ½ cups almond milk
- 1 banana, peeled and sliced
- 1/3 cup frozen cherries
- 1/3 cup fresh blueberries
- 1/4 teaspoon vanilla extract
- 1 tablespoon vegan protein powder, zero carbs

Directions

Mix all ingredients in your blender or a smoothie maker until creamy and uniform.

Serve in individual glasses and enjoy!

Nutritional Information

247 Calories;
21.7g Fat;
4.9g Carbs;
2.6g Protein;
1.8g Fiber

4 Servings   **25 minutes**

3. Southwest-Inspired Tofu Scramble

Ingredients

- 2 tablespoons olive oil
- 1 (14-ounce) block tofu, pressed and cubed
- 1 celery stalk, chopped
- 1 bunch scallions, chopped
- 1 teaspoon cayenne pepper
- 1 teaspoon garlic powder
- 2 tablespoons Worcestershire sauce
- Salt and black pepper, to taste
- 1 pound Brussels sprouts, trimmed and quartered
- 1/2 teaspoon turmeric powder
- 1/2 teaspoon dried sill weed
- 1/4 teaspoon dried basil

Directions

Heat 1 tablespoon of olive oil in a large-sized skillet over a moderately high flame. Add the tofu cubes and cook, gently stirring, for 8 minutes.

Now, add the celery and scallions; cook until they are softened, about 5 minutes

Add the cayenne pepper, garlic powder, Worcestershire sauce, salt, and pepper; continue to cook for 3 more minutes; reserve.

Heat the remaining 1 tablespoon of oil in the same pan. Cook the Brussels sprouts along with the remaining seasonings for 4 minutes. Add the tofu mixture to the Brussels sprouts and serve warm. Enjoy!

Nutritional Information

128 Calories;
8.3g Fat;
 6.5g Carbs;
5.1g Protein;
5.1g Fiber

4. American-Style Chocolate Pancakes

6 Servings   20 minutes

Ingredients

- 1 ½ cups almond flour
- 1 ½ teaspoon baking powder
- 2 tablespoons Swerve
- 1/2 cup full-fat coconut milk
- A pinch of kosher salt
- 1/2 teaspoon pure coconut extract
- 1/2 teaspoon pure vanilla extract
- 1 cup pumpkin puree, unsweetened, preferably homemade
- 1 ½ tablespoons fresh lime juice
- 2 tablespoons cocoa powder, unsweetened

Directions

Pulse all ingredients in a blender or a food processor until you have a smooth batter. Let the batter stand for 10 minutes.

Heat a lightly oiled griddle over medium-high heat. Scoop the batter onto the griddle, using approximately 1/4 cup for each pancake. Brown for 2 to 3 minutes per side.

Repeat until you run out of batter. Serve hot and enjoy!

Nutritional Information

196 Calories;
16.8g Fat;
7.5g Carbs;
6.1g Protein;
3.5g Fiber

8 Servings   **1 hour**

5. Multi Nut and Seed Granola

Ingredients

- 2 tablespoons coconut oil
- 1/3 cup coconut flakes
- 1 ½ cups coconut milk
- 2 tablespoons sugar
- 1/8 teaspoon Himalayan salt
- 1 teaspoon orange zest
- 1/8 teaspoon nutmeg, freshly grated
- 1/2 teaspoon ground cinnamon
- 1/2 cup walnuts, chopped
- 1/2 cup almonds, slivered
- 2 tablespoons pepitas
- 2 tablespoons sunflower seeds
- 1/4 cup flax seed

Directions

Warm the coconut oil in a deep pan that is preheated over a moderately high flame. Toast the coconut flakes for 1 to 2 minutes.

Add the remaining ingredients; stir to combine.

Preheat your oven to 300 degrees F. Spread the mixture out in an even layer onto a parchment lined baking sheet.

Bake for 1 hour, gently tossing every 15 minutes. Serve with some extra coconut milk. Bon appétit!

Nutritional Information

262 Calories
24.3g Fat
5.2g Carbs
5.1g Protein
2.8g Fiber

6. Chia, Blackberry and Cocoa Smoothie

2 Servings   5 minutes

Ingredients

- 1 cup blackberries
- 1 cup water
- 1 tablespoon chia seeds
- 1 tablespoon cocoa
- 1/4 teaspoon ground nutmeg
- 1 tablespoon peanut butter
- Liquid Stevia, to taste

Directions

Add all ingredients to your blender or a food processor.

Mix until creamy and uniform. Pour into two tall glasses and serve immediately. Enjoy!

Nutritional Information

103 Calories
5.9g Fat
6.1g Carbs
4.1g Protein
4.6g Fiber

7. The Ultimate Home-made Sandwich Rolls

8 Servings

1 hour

Ingredients

- 1 ½ cups almond flour
- 1/4 cup flaxseed meal
- 1/4 cup coconut flour
- 1/3 cup ground psyllium husk
- 1 teaspoon sea salt
- 1 tablespoon baking powder
- 1/2 teaspoon baking soda
- 2 tablespoons olive oil
- 1 ½ tablespoons cider vinegar
- 1 1/3 cups hot water

Nutritional Information

143 Calories
13.2g Fat
4.2g Carbs
4.1g Protein
2.5g Fiber

Directions

Start by preheating your oven to 370 degrees F. Coat a baking pan with parchment paper and set aside.

In a mixing bowl, thoroughly combine the dry ingredients. Then, in another bowl, mix the wet ingredients.

Add the dry mixture to the wet mixture and mix until you are able to form a ball with your hands. Your dough should be elastic and soft.

Let it sit for 10 to 12 minutes; shape the dough into 8 balls. Roll each ball between your wet hands; arrange them on the pre-pared baking pan.

Bake in the preheated oven approximately 45 minutes. Transfer to a cooling rack before serving. Bon appétit!

8. Hemp Heart Porridge with Strawberries

4 Servings   **5 minutes + chiling time**

Ingredients

- 1/2 cup water
- 1/2 cup unsweetened almond milk
- 3/4 cup hemp hearts
- 6 drops of liquid stevia
- 1/4 teaspoon ground cloves
- 1/4 teaspoon ground cinnamon
- 1 cup strawberries, halved

Directions

- Combine all ingredients, except for the strawberries, in an airtight container.
- Cover and place in your refrigerator overnight.
- In the morning, top with fresh strawberries and serve immediately.

Nutritional Information

176 Calories

12.7g Fat

5g Carbs

9.7g Protein

1.3g Fiber

12 Servings   **40 minutes**

9. Gooey Pumpkin Muffins

Ingredients

- 2/3 cup smooth peanut butter
- 1/3 cup sesame butter
- 1 cup pumpkin puree
- 1/3 cup monk fruit sweetener
- 1 teaspoon baking powder
- 1/4 teaspoon ground cinnamon
- 1/4 teaspoon ground cardamom
- 1/3 cup cocoa powder

Directions

In a mixing bowl, thoroughly combine all ingredients until everything is well combined. Then, spoon the batter into a lightly greased muffin tin.

Bake in the preheated oven at 355 degrees F for about 25 minutes.

Transfer to a cooling rack and let them sit for 10 minutes before serving. Bon appétit!

Nutritional Information

99 Calories
6.5g Fat
6.2g Carbs
3.2g Protein
1.6g Fiber

10. Home-Style Hazelnut "Cereal"

4 Servings   10 minutes

Ingredients

- 2 tablespoons coconut oil
- 1/3 cup coconut shreds
- 2 ½ cups coconut milk, full-fat
- 1/2 cup water
- 2 tablespoons confectioners' erythritol
- 1/8 teaspoon salt
- 1/2 teaspoon vanilla paste
- 1/2 cup flax seed
- 16 hazelnuts, roughly chopped

Directions

Melt the coconut oil in a pan over a moderate heat. Then, add the coconut shreds, coconut milk, water, confectioners' erythritol, salt, vanilla paste, and flax seed.

Simmer for 5 minutes, stirring periodically. Allow it to cool down slightly.

Then, ladle into four individual bowls. Serve topped with chopped hazelnuts. Bon appétit!

Nutritional Information

79 Calories
23.6g Fat
5.9g Carbs
7.2g Protein
5.2g Fiber

11. 1-Minute Muffin in a Mug

Ingredients

- 2 tablespoons coconut flour
- 1 tablespoon almond flour
- 1 tablespoon granulated stevia
- 1/2 teaspoon baking powder
- 1/4 teaspoon ground cinnamon
- 1/8 teaspoon grated nutmeg
- 1 flax egg (1 tablespoon of flax seeds mixed with 2 tablespoons of water)
- 1 tablespoon coconut oil
- 2 tablespoons coconut milk
- 2 tablespoon cranberries

Nutritional Information

273 Calories
26g Fat
7.7g Carbs
2.8g Protein
4.7g Fiber

Directions

In a mixing bowl, thoroughly combine the flours, sweetener, baking powder, cinnamon, and nutmeg.

Add in the flax egg, coconut oil, and milk; mix to combine well. Fold in the cranberries and mix again. Spoon the mixture into a mug.

Microwave for 1 minute and serve immediately. Enjoy!

12. Raspberry Peanut Butter Shake

1 Servings   5 minutes

Ingredients

- 1/3 cup raspberries
- 1/2 cup baby spinach leaves
- 3/4 cup almond milk, unsweetened
- 1 tablespoon peanut butter
- 1 teaspoon Swerve

Directions

Place all ingredients in your blender and puree until creamy, uniform and smooth.

Pour into a tall glass. Serve well-chilled.

Nutritional Information

114 Calories
8.2g Fat
7.9g Carbs
4.2g Protein
3.4g Fiber

6 Servings 1 hour

13. Keto Breakfast Crunch

Ingredients

- 1/2 cup pecans, chopped
- 1 cup walnuts, chopped
- 1/3 cup flax meal
- 1/3 cup coconut milk
- 1/3 cup sesame seeds
- 1/3 cup pumpkin seeds
- 8 drops stevia
- 1/3 cup coconut oil, melted
- 1 ½ teaspoons vanilla paste
- 1 teaspoon ground cloves
- 1 teaspoon freshly grated nutmeg
- 1 teaspoon orange zest
- 1/3 cup water

Nutritional Information

449 Calories
44.9g Fat
6.2g Carbs
9.3g Protein
3.2g Fiber

Directions

Begin by preheating your oven to 300 degrees F. Line a baking sheet with parchment paper.

Mix all ingredients until well combined. Now, spread this mixture out in an even layer onto the prepared baking sheet.

Bake about 55 minutes, stirring every 15 minutes. Allow it to cool down at room temperature.

Afterwards, transfer to an airtight container or serve immediately. Bon appétit!

14. Autumn Chia Pudding

3 Servings   5 minutes + prep time

Ingredients

- 2 cups almond milk, unsweetened
- 1/2 cup chia seeds
- 1/2 teaspoon vanilla extract
- 1/4 teaspoon cardamom
- 1/4 teaspoon ground cinnamon
- A pinch of salt
- 2 teaspoons Swerve, powdered
- 8 plums, pitted and halved

Directions

Place all of the above ingredients, except for the Swerve and plums, in an airtight container.

Allow it to stand, covered, in your refrigerator overnight.

Sweeten with the powdered Swerve and serve well-chilled with fresh plums. Enjoy!

Nutritional Information

153 Calories
8g Fat
10.7g Carbs
6.7g Protein
8.2g Fiber

2 Servings **5 minutes**

15. Butternut Squash and Cocoa Bowl

Ingredients

- 2 ½ cups almond milk
- 1/2 cup baby spinach
- 2 tablespoons cocoa powder
- 1/2 cup butternut squash, roasted
- 1/2 teaspoon ground cinnamon
- A pinch of grated nutmeg
- A pinch of salt

Directions

Mix all ingredients in a blender or a food processor.

Serve well-chilled in tall glasses. Enjoy!

Nutritional Information

71 Calories
2.3g Fat
4.1g Carbs
4.3g Protein
3.1g Fiber

SOUPS & STEWS

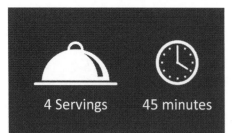

16. Thick Zucchini Soup

4 Servings　　**45 minutes**

Ingredients

- 3 teaspoons vegetable oil
- 1 yellow onion, chopped
- 1 carrot, sliced
- 1 parsnip, sliced
- 3 cups zucchini, peeled and chopped
- 1/4 teaspoon ground black pepper
- 4 cups water
- 1 tablespoon vegetable bouillon powder
- 1 tomato, pureed
- 1 avocado pitted, peeled and diced

Nutritional Information

165 Calories
13.4g Fat
6.7g Carbs
2.2g Protein
5.5g Fiber

Directions

Heat the oil in a heavy-bottomed pot that is preheated over a moderate heat. Now, sweat the onions until they are softened.

Add the carrot, parsnip, and zucchini and cook for 7 more minutes; season with black pepper. Reserve the vegetables.

After that, add the water, vegetable bouillon powder, and pureed tomato; bring it to a rapid boil. Turn the heat to medium-low and let it simmer for 18 minutes.

Add the reserved vegetables and simmer for a further 18 minutes. Remove from heat and stir in the avocado.

Blend the soup in batches until smooth and creamy.

17. Hungarian-Style Chanterelle Stew

4 Servings　　**25 minutes**

Ingredients

- 2 tablespoons olive oil
- 1 cup leeks, chopped
- 2 garlic cloves, pressed
- 1/2 cup celery with leaves, chopped
- 2 carrots, chopped
- 1 cup fresh Chanterelle, sliced
- 2 tablespoons dry red wine
- 2 rosemary sprigs, chopped
- 1 thyme sprig, chopped
- 3 ½ cups roasted vegetable stock
- 1/2 teaspoon cayenne pepper
- 1 teaspoon Hungarian paprika
- 2 ripe tomatoes, pureed
- 1 tablespoon flaxseed meal

Directions

Heat the oil in a stockpot over a moderate flame. Now, cook the leeks until they are tender.

Add the garlic, celery, and carrots and cook for a further 4 minutes or until they are softened.

Now, stir in the Chanterelle mushrooms; cook until they lose their liquid; reserve the vegetables.

Pour in the wine to deglaze the bottom of the stockpot. Now, add the rosemary and thyme.

Add the roasted vegetable stock, cayenne pepper, Hungarian paprika, and tomatoes; stir in reserved vegetables and bring to a boil.

Reduce heat to a simmer. Let it simmer, covered, an additional 15 minutes. Add the flaxseed meal to thicken the soup. Serve in individual soup bowls with a few sprinkles of Hungarian paprika.

Nutritional Information

114 Calories
7.3g Fat
5.2g Carbs
2.1g Protein
3.8g Fiber

4 Servings   **15 minutes**

18. Silky Broccoli Soup

Ingredients

- 2 tablespoons coconut oil, at room temperature
- 2 shallots, finely chopped
- 1 teaspoon garlic, minced
- 1 pound broccoli, cut into small florets
- 8 ounces kale leaves, torn into small pieces
- 4 cups vegetable broth
- 1/2 cup almond milk
- 1/2 teaspoon kosher salt
- 1/2 teaspoon crushed red pepper flakes
- 2 tablespoons chives, coarsely chopped

Directions

Heat the coconut oil in a pot that is preheated over a moderate flame. Then, sauté the shallots and garlic until they're fragrant and slightly browned.

Now, add the broccoli, kale and vegetable broth; bring to a boil for 5 minutes.

Pour in the almond milk, salt and pepper; cover and let your soup simmer over a moderate flame.

Afterwards, blend the soup with an immersion blender; serve right away garnished with fresh chopped chives!

Nutritional Information

252 Calories
20.3g Fat
6.8g Carbs
8.1g Protein
5.3g Fiber

19. Japanese-Style Soup with Greens

6 Servings   25 minutes

Ingredients

- 2 teaspoons olive oil
- 1 shallot, chopped
- 2 cloves garlic, minced
- 1 celery stalk, chopped
- 1 zucchini, chopped
- 1 carrot, sliced
- 1 cup kale, torn into pieces
- 1 cup mustard greens, torn into pieces
- Sea salt and ground black pepper, to taste
- 2 thyme sprigs, chopped
- 1 rosemary sprig, chopped
- 2 bay leaves
- 6 cups vegetable stock
- 2 ripe tomatoes, chopped
- 1 cup almond milk, unflavored
- 1 tablespoon white miso paste
- 1/2 cup watercress

Directions

Heat the olive oil in a large pot that is pre-heated over a moderately high heat. Now, sauté the shallots, garlic, celery, zucchini, and carrots until they're softened.

Now, add the kale, mustard greens, salt, ground black pepper, thyme, rosemary, bay leaves, vegetable stock and tomatoes.

Reduce the heat to simmer. Let it simmer another 15 minutes, leaving the lid slightly ajar.

After that, add the almond milk, white miso paste, and watercress. Cook an additional 5 minutes, stirring periodically. Bon appétit!

Nutritional Information

142 Calories
11.4g Fat
5.6g Carbs
2.9g Protein
1.3g Fiber

4 Servings **50 minutes**

20. Classic Mushroom Stroganoff

Ingredients

- 2 teaspoons olive oil
- 1 yellow onion, chopped
- 1 garlic clove, finely minced
- 1/2 cup celery, chopped
- 1/2 cup carrot, chopped
- 1 green bell pepper, chopped
- 1 jalapeno pepper, chopped
- 2 ½ cups white mushrooms, thinly sliced
- 1 ½ cups vegetable stock
- 2 ripe tomatoes, chopped
- 2 thyme sprigs, chopped
- 1 rosemary sprig, chopped
- 2 bay leaves
- 1/2 teaspoon salt
- 1/4 teaspoon ground black pepper, or more to taste
- 1/4 teaspoon grated nutmeg
- 2 tablespoons apple cider vinegar

Directions

Heat the oil in a pot that is preheated over a moderately high heat. Now, sauté the onions and garlic until tender and fragrant.

Stir in the celery, carrots, pepper, and mushrooms. Cook for 12 minutes more, stirring periodically; add a splash of vegetable stock to prevent sticking.

Add the remaining ingredients, except for the apple cider vinegar.

Turn the heat to medium-low; let it simmer for 25 to 35 minutes or until everything is thoroughly cooked.

Ladle into individual bowls, drizzle each serving with apple cider vinegar and eat warm.

Nutritional Information

65 Calories
2.7g Fat
6g Carbs
2.7g Protein
2.3g Fiber

21. Simple Cauliflower Soup

4 Servings   20 minutes

Ingredients

- 4 cups water
- 2 heads of cauliflower, broken into florets
- 1 ½ tablespoons vegetable bouillon granules
- 1/4 teaspoon ground bay leaves
- 1/4 teaspoon ground cloves
- 2 tablespoons extra-virgin olive oil
- 1/2 teaspoon red pepper flakes

Directions

In a heavy-bottomed pot, bring the water to a boil over a moderately high heat.

Stir in the cauliflower florets; cook for 10 minutes.

Add the bouillon granules, ground bay leaves, and ground cloves. Now, reduce the heat to medium-low; continue to cook for 5 minutes longer.

Puree this mixture by using a food processor or an immersion blender.

Divide among four soup bowl; drizzle each serving with olive oil and sprinkle with red pepper. Eat warm.

Nutritional Information

94 Calories
7.2g Fat
5.5g Carbs
2.7g Protein
2.7g Fiber

3 Servings   **25 minutes**

22. Mom's Cabbage Stew

Ingredients

- 2 tablespoons olive oil
- 1 yellow onion, diced
- 2 garlic cloves, minced
- 1 pound green cabbage, shredded
- 2 cups tomato puree
- 1 cup vegetable stock
- 2 bay leaves
- 1/2 teaspoon red pepper flakes, crushed
- Sea salt and freshly cracked black pepper, to taste

Directions

Heat the olive oil in a non-stick skillet over medium heat. Now, sauté the onion until just tender and translucent. Sit in the garlic and continue to sauté an additional minute.

Cook the cabbage in a stock pot with the tomato puree, vegetable stock, and bay leaves; cook until it is just tender, about 10 minutes.

Stir the sautéed mixture into the warm cabbage; stir in the red pepper, salt, and black pepper. Cover the pot and let it simmer over medium-low heat for 7 minutes more. Serve immediately.

Nutritional Information

134 Calories
7.7g Fat
9.1g Carbs
3.7g Protein
4.2g Fiber

23. Persian Stew (Khoresht Badam)

4 Servings　　**15 minutes**

Ingredients

- 4 tablespoons olive oil
- 1 (12-ounce) pack firm tofu cut into cubes
- 1 leek, chopped
- 1 teaspoon ginger garlic paste
- 1/2 teaspoon cayenne pepper
- Sea salt and ground black pepper, to taste
- 4 tablespoons almond butter
- 1 cup warm water
- 2 vegan bouillon cubes
- 1 teaspoon hot sauce
- 1 vine-ripe tomato, chopped
- 1/2 teaspoon ground cumin
- A pinch of grated nutmeg
- 1 tablespoon fresh Italian parsley, chopped

Directions

Heat 2 tablespoons of olive oil in a saucepan over medium-high heat; then, brown the tofu cubes for 3 to 5 minutes on all sides; reserve.

Heat the remaining 2 tablespoons of olive oil and sauté the leeks until tender and fragrant; add the ginger garlic paste, cayenne pepper, salt, and black pepper.

Next, thoroughly combine the almond butter with water, bouillon cubes, hot sauce, chopped tomato, cumin, and nutmeg.

Add this mixture to the pan along with the reserved tofu cubes. Allow it to cook for 2 to 4 minutes or until thoroughly heated. Garnish with fresh parsley leaves and serve hot!

Nutritional Information

333 Calories
30.4g Fat
5.6g Carbs
9.8g Protein
1.4g Fiber

4 Servings

1 hour 20 minutes

24. Mediterranean Eggplant Soup

Ingredients

- 1 pound eggplant, cut it in half.
- 2 ripe tomatoes, chopped
- 2 shallots, chopped
- 2 garlic cloves, peeled
- 1 tablespoon olive oil
- 1/2 teaspoon dried oregano
- 1/2 teaspoon dried basil
- 1/2 teaspoon dried marjoram
- 3 cups water
- 3 vegan bouillon cubes
- 1/3 cup raw cashews, soaked
- Salt and pepper, to taste

Nutritional Information

159 Calories
9.4g Fat
7.1g Carbs
4.2g Protein
5.1g Fiber

Directions

Start by preheating your oven to 390 degrees F.

Arrange the eggplant on a parchment lined baking sheet. Drizzle olive oil over the eggplant.

Roast about 35 to 40 minutes or until tender. Scoop the eggplant from the skin and transfer to a pot.

Add the remaining ingredient, except for the cashews. Let it simmer, covered, for 40 minutes. Puree the soup with a hand blender.

Drain your cashews and blend them with 1 cup water in a blender until smooth. Add the cashew cream to the soup; stir well and serve immediately.

25. Nana's Cream of Cauliflower Soup

4 Servings   25 minutes

Ingredients

- 1 tablespoon almond oil
- 1 cup shallots, chopped
- 1 celery with leaves, chopped
- 2 cloves garlic, minced
- 1 head cauliflower, broken into florets
- 4 cups water
- Salt and white pepper, to taste
- 1/4 cup ground almonds
- 1 tablespoon fresh parsley, chopped

Directions

Heat the oil in a stockpot that is preheated over a moderate heat. Now, sauté the shallots, celery and garlic until tender, about 6 minutes.

Add the cauliflower, water, salt, and white pepper. Add the ground almonds.

Bring to a boil; then, reduce the heat to low; continue to simmer for about 17 minutes.

Next, puree the soup with an immersion blender. Serve garnished with fresh parsley. Bon appétit!

Nutritional Information

114 Calories
6.5g Fat
5.1g Carbs
3.8g Protein
1.7g Fiber

SALADS

26. Greek-Style Salad

4 Servings

3 hours
15 minutes

Ingredients

For Sunflower Seed Dressing:
- 1 cup sunflower seeds, raw and hulled
- 2 cups water
- 2 tablespoons scallions, chopped
- 1 garlic clove, chopped
- 1 lime, freshly squeezed
- Salt and black pepper, to taste
- 1/2 teaspoon red pepper flakes crushed
- 1/4 teaspoon rosemary, minced
- 2 tablespoons coconut milk

For the salad:
- 1 head fresh lettuce, separated into leaves
- 3 tomatoes, diced
- 3 cucumbers, sliced
- 2 tablespoons Kalamata olives, pitted

Nutritional Information

208 Calories
15.6g Fat
6.2g Carbs
7.6g Protein
5.1g Fiber

Directions

Soak the sunflower seeds in water at least 3 hours. Drain the sunflower seeds; transfer them to your blender and add the remaining ingredients for the dressing.

Puree until creamy, smooth and uniform.

Put all the salad ingredients into four serving bowls. Toss with the dressing and serve immediately. Bon appétit!

4 Servings 10 minutes

27. Moroccan Carrot Salad with Harissa

Ingredients

- 1 pound carrots, coarsely shredded
- 1/4 cup fresh cilantro, chopped
- For the Vinaigrette:
- 3 garlic cloves, smashed
- Sea salt and ground black pepper, to taste
- 1/3 cup extra-virgin olive oil
- 1 lime, freshly squeezed
- 2 tablespoons balsamic vinegar
- 1/2 teaspoon ground cumin
- 1/2 teaspoon harissa

Nutritional Information

196 Calories
17.2g Fat
6g Carbs
1.2g Protein
3.5g Fiber

Directions

Place the shredded carrots and fresh, chopped cilantro in a salad bowl.

Combine all ingredients for the vinaigrette; mix until everything is well incorporated.

Add the vinaigrette to the carrot salad and toss to coat well. Bon appétit!

28. Warm Savoy Cabbage Slaw

4 Servings | 25 minutes

Ingredients

- 2 pounds Savoy cabbage, torn into pieces
- 2 tablespoons almond oil
- 1 teaspoon garlic, minced
- 1/2 teaspoon dried basil
- 1/2 teaspoon red pepper flakes, crushed
- Salt and ground black pepper, to the taste

Directions

Cook the Savoy cabbage in a pot of a lightly salted water approximately 20 minutes over a moderate heat. Drain and reserve.

Now, heat the oil in a sauté pan over a medium-high heat. Now, cook the garlic until just aromatic.

Add the reserved Savoy cabbage, basil, red pepper, salt and black pepper; stir until everything is heated through.

Taste, adjust the seasonings and serve warm over cauliflower rice.

Nutritional Information

118 Calories
7g Fat
6.7g Carbs
2.9g Protein
5g Fiber

4 Servings   **25 minutes**

29. Taco Salad Boats

Ingredients

- 1 head romaine lettuce, stems removed
- 1/2 cup canned black beans
- 1 cup tomatoes, chopped
- 1 medium bunch of scallions, sliced
- 2 peppers, shredded
- 1 cup red cabbage, shredded
- 1 ripe avocado, peeled, pitted and diced
- 1/2 cup sesame butter
- 1 tablespoon apple cider vinegar
- 1 tablespoon fresh lime juice
- 1 teaspoon chili powder
- Sea salt and ground black pepper, to taste
- 1/2 red pepper flakes

Directions

Pull the leaves off of the romaine hearts and arrange them on a tray.

In a mixing bowl, combine the black beans with the tomatoes, scallions, peppers, red cabbage, and avocado. Fill the romaine "boats" with the bean mixture.

Then, mix the sesame butter with the apple cider vinegar, lime juice, chili powder, salt, and black pepper. Drizzle the sauce over the filling.

Garnish with red pepper flakes and serve immediately. Bon appétit!

Nutritional Information

140 Calories
10.8g Fat
7.2g Carbs
4.3g Protein
5g Fiber

30. Cauliflower Salad with Pecans

4 Servings

15 minutes + chilling time

Ingredients

- 1 head fresh cauliflower, cut into florets
- 1 cup spring onions, chopped
- 4 ounces bottled roasted peppers, chopped
- 1/4 cup extra-virgin olive oil
- 1 tablespoon wine vinegar
- 1 teaspoon yellow mustard
- Coarse salt and black pepper, to your liking
- 1/2 cup green olives, pitted and chopped
- 1/2 cup pecans, coarsely chopped

Directions

Steam the cauliflower florets for 4 to 6 minutes; set aside to cool.

In a salad bowl, place the spring onions and roasted peppers.

In a mixing dish, whisk the olive oil, vinegar, mustard, salt and pepper. Drizzle over the veggies in the salad bowl.

Now, add the reserved cauliflower and toss to combine well. Scatter the green olives and pecans over the top and serve.

Nutritional Information

281 Calories
26.8g Fat
5.6g Carbs
4.2g Protein
3.8g Fiber

31. Crunchy Broccoli Salad

Ingredients

- 1 pound frozen broccoli, thawed and broken into small florets
- 1 cup green onions, chopped
- 1 bell pepper, sliced
- 1/4 cup pecan, slivered
- 1/3 cup extra-virgin olive oil
- 2 tablespoons balsamic vinegar
- 1/2 teaspoon basil
- 1/2 teaspoon oregano
- Sea salt and freshly ground black pepper

Nutritional Information

245 Calories
22.8g Fat
6g Carbs
4.2g Protein
4.3g Fiber

Directions

Thoroughly combine all ingredients in a salad bowl.

Cover and let it sit in your refrigerator until ready to serve. Bon appétit!

32. Kale Salad with Crispy Tofu Cubes

4 Servings   15 minutes

Ingredients

- 2 tablespoons coconut oil
- 1 (14-ounce) block extra-firm tofu, pressed and cubed
- 1 bunch kale, torn into small pieces
- 1 shallot, sliced
- 1 garlic clove, pressed
- 1/4 cup cilantro leaves, divided
- 1 jalapeno pepper, seeded and minced
- 1/4 cup olive oil
- 1 lemon, juices
- Sea salt and ground black pepper, to taste
- 1 (1-inch) piece fresh ginger, peeled and grated
- 1 tablespoon coconut aminos
- 1 tablespoon sunflower seeds, lightly toasted
- 1 tablespoon pumpkin seeds, lightly toasted

Directions

Heat the coconut oil in a saucepan over medium heat; now, cook the tofu cubes until they are golden brown on all sides. Reserve.

Mix the kale, shallot, garlic, cilantro, and jalapeno pepper in a salad bowl; then, drizzle the salad with olive oil and lemon juice.

Add the salt, pepper, ginger, and coconut aminos; toss to combine well. Top with the reserved tofu cubes. Scatter lightly toasted seeds over your salad and serve.

Nutritional Information

327 Calories
29.1g Fat
7.2g Carbs
13.2g Protein
3.7g Fiber

4 Servings   15 minutes

33. Cucumber and Zucchini Ribbon Salad

Ingredients

- 2 medium cucumbers, julienned
- 2 medium zucchinis, julienned
- 1 teaspoon sea salt
- 2 tomatoes, sliced
- 1 white onion, chopped
- 1 cup rocket lettuce, torn into pieces
- 1/3 cup extra-virgin olive oil
- 1 teaspoon fresh garlic, pressed
- 2 tablespoons balsamic vinegar
- 1 tablespoon Dijon mustard
- Sea salt and ground black pepper, to taste
- 2 tablespoons sesame seeds, lightly toasted
- 2 tablespoons sunflower seeds, lightly toasted

Directions

Toss the cucumber and zucchini with 1 teaspoon of sea salt in a fine mesh sieve; place the sieve over the bowl.

Let it sit for about 20 minutes; then, squeeze the cucumber and zucchini gently to remove any excess liquid. Transfer them to a large bowl.

Add in the tomatoes, onion, and rocket lettuce. Make the vinaigrette by whisking the olive oil, garlic, balsamic vinegar, mustard, salt, and black pepper to taste.

Dress your salad and serve garnished with lightly toasted seeds. Eat immediately or place in your refrigerator until ready to serve!

Nutritional Information

252 Calories
23.1g Fat
6.1g Carbs
3.5g Protein
2.7g Fiber

MAIN COURSE

4 Servings   40 minutes

34. Sriracha Tofu with Greek Tzatziki Sauce

Ingredients

- 12 ounces tofu, pressed and cut into 1/4-inch thick slices
- 1 cup scallions, chopped
- 1 garlic clove, minced
- 2 tablespoons champagne vinegar
- 1 tablespoon Sriracha sauce
- 2 tablespoons sesame oil

For Vegan Tzatziki:
- 2 cloves garlic, pressed
- 2 tablespoons fresh lemon juice
- Sea salt and ground black pepper, to taste
- 1 teaspoon fresh or dried dill weed
- 1 cup non-dairy yogurt
- 1 cucumber, shredded

Directions

Place the tofu slices, scallions, garlic, vinegar, and Sriracha sauce in a bowl; let it stand for 30 minutes.

Heat the oil in a nonstick skillet over medium-high heat. Cook the tofu until it is golden brown, about 5 minutes.

To make the vegan tzatziki, thoroughly combine the garlic, lemon juice, salt, black pepper, dill and yogurt in a mixing bowl.

Stir in the shredded cucumber; stir until everything is well incorporated.

Place the tzatziki in the refrigerator until ready to serve. Divide the tofu among serving plates and serve with a dollop of tzatziki. Enjoy!

Nutritional Information

162 Calories
10.9g Fat
5.8g Carbs
9.5g Protein
4.7g Fiber

35. Spicy Tofu with Peppers

2 Servings　　**40 minutes**

Ingredients

- 12 ounces extra firm tofu, pressed and cubed
- 1 ½ tablespoons flaxseed meal
- Salt and ground black pepper, to taste
- 1 teaspoon garlic paste
- 1/2 teaspoon paprika
- 1 teaspoon shallot powder
- 1/2 teaspoon ground bay leaf
- 1 tablespoon olive oil
- 1 red bell pepper, deveined and sliced
- 1 green bell pepper, deveined and sliced
- 1 serrano pepper, deveined and sliced

Directions

Place the tofu, flaxseed meal, salt, black pepper, garlic paste, paprika, shallot powder, and ground bay leaf in a container.

Cover, toss to coat, and let it marinate at least 30 minutes.

Heat the olive oil in a saucepan over a moderate heat. Cook your tofu along with the peppers for 5 to 7 minutes, gently stirring.

Serve immediately and enjoy!

Nutritional Information

223 Calories
15.9g Fat
5.1g Carbs
15.6g Protein
4.2g Fiber

36. Curried Oven-Roasted Cauliflower

4 Servings　　**35 minutes**

Ingredients

- 1 pound cauliflower, broken into florets
- 2 bell peppers, halved
- 2 pasilla peppers, halved
- 1/4 cup extra-virgin olive oil
- 1/2 teaspoon sea salt
- 1/4 teaspoon freshly ground black pepper, or more to taste
- 1/2 teaspoon cayenne pepper
- 1 teaspoon curry powder
- 1/2 teaspoon nigella seeds

Directions

Preheat your oven to 425 degrees F. Line a large baking sheet with a piece of parchment paper.

Drizzle the cauliflower and peppers with extra-virgin olive oil. Sprinkle with salt, black pepper, cayenne pepper, curry powder and nigella seeds

Next, arrange the vegetables on the prepared baking sheet.

Roast the vegetables, tossing periodically, until they are slightly browned, about 30 minutes.

Serve with a homemade tomato dip or mushroom pate. Bon appétit!

Nutritional Information

166 Calories
13.9g Fat
5.4g Carbs
3g Protein
3.9g Fiber

37. Saucy Tempeh with Brussels Sprouts

4 Servings   20 minutes

Ingredients

- 2 tablespoons olive oil
- 2 garlic cloves, minced
- 1/2 cup leeks, chopped
- 10 ounces tempeh, crumbled
- 2 tablespoons water
- 2 tablespoons soy sauce
- 1 tablespoon tomato puree
- 1/2 pound Brussels sprouts, quartered
- Sea salt and ground black pepper, to taste

Directions

Heat the oil in a saucepan that is preheated over a moderate heat. Now, cook the garlic and leeks until tender and aromatic.

Now, add the tempeh, water and soy sauce. Cook until the tempeh just begins to brown, about 5 minutes.

Stir in the shredded cabbage; season with salt and pepper; turn the heat to low and cook, stirring often, for about 13 minutes. Serve warm.

Nutritional Information

179 Calories
11.7g Fat
3.1g Carbs
10.5g Protein
2.6g Fiber

4 Servings　　**15 minutes**

38. Guilt-Free Parmesan Zoodles

Ingredients

For Zoodles:

- 4 zucchinis, peeled
- 2 tablespoons olive oil
- 1/2 cup water
- Salt and cayenne pepper, to taste
- For Cashew Parmesan:
- 1/2 cup raw cashews
- 2 tablespoons nutritional yeast
- Sea salt and black pepper, to taste
- 1/4 teaspoon shallot powder
- 1/2 teaspoon garlic powder

Directions

Slice the zucchinis into long strips i.e. noodle-shape strands.

Heat the oil in a pan over medium heat; cook the zucchini for 1 minute or so, stirring continuously. Pour in the water and cook 6 more minutes. Season with salt and cayenne pepper to taste.

Then, pulse all the parmesan ingredients in your food processor until you reach a Parmesan cheese consistency.

Top the cooked zoodles with the cashew parmesan and enjoy!

Nutritional Information

145 Calories
10.6g Fat
4.9g Carbs
5.5g Protein
1.6g Fiber

39. Easy Fried Tofu with Pecans

4 Servings　**13 minutes**

Ingredients

- 3 teaspoons olive oil
- 1 cup extra firm tofu, pressed and cubed
- 1/4 cup pecans, coarsely chopped
- 1 ½ tablespoons soy sauce
- 3 tablespoons vegetable broth
- 1/2 teaspoon granulated garlic
- 1 teaspoon cayenne pepper
- 1/2 teaspoon turmeric powder
- Sea salt and ground black pepper, to taste
- 2 teaspoons sunflower seeds

Directions

Heat the oil in a frying pan that is preheated over a moderate heat. Once hot, fry the tofu cubes until golden brown, stirring periodically.

Stir in the pecans; increase the temperature and cook on high for 2 minutes or until fragrant.

Add the remaining ingredients, reduce the heat to medium-low and cook an additional 5 minutes.

Serve drizzled with hot sauce and enjoy!

Nutritional Information

232 Calories
21.6g Fat
5.3g Carbs
8.3g Protein
2.7g Fiber

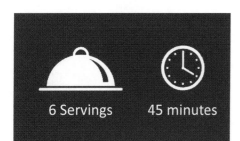

6 Servings

45 minutes

40. Asparagus with Lebanese Baba Ghanoush

Ingredients

- 1 ½ pounds asparagus spears, trim and cut off the woody ends
- 1/4 cup olive oil
- 1 teaspoon sea salt
- 1/2 teaspoon ground black pepper, to taste
- 1/2 teaspoon paprika

For Baba Ghanoush:
- 3/4 pound eggplant
- 2 teaspoons olive oil
- 1/2 cup scallions, chopped
- 2 cloves garlic, minced
- 1 tablespoon tahini
- 2 tablespoons fresh lemon juice
- 1/2 teaspoon cayenne pepper
- Salt and ground black pepper, to taste
- 1/4 cup fresh parsley leaves, chopped

Nutritional Information

149 Calories
12.1g Fat
6.3g Carbs
3.6g Protein
4.9g Fiber

Directions

Begin by preheating your oven to 390 degrees F. Line a baking sheet with parchment paper.

Place the asparagus spears on the baking sheet.

Toss the asparagus spears with the oil, salt, pepper, and paprika. Bake about 9 minutes or until thoroughly cooked.

Then, make the Baba Ghanoush. Preheat your oven to 425 degrees F.

Place the eggplants on a lined cookie sheet. Set under the broiler approximately 30 minutes; allow the eggplants to cool. Now, peel the eggplants and remove the stems.

Heat 2 teaspoons of olive oil in a frying pan over a moderately high flame. Now, sauté the scallions and garlic until tender and aromatic.

Add the roasted eggplant, scallion mixture, tahini, lemon juice, cayenne pepper, salt and black pepper to your food processor. Pulse until the ingredients are evenly mixed.

Garnish with parsley and serve with the roasted asparagus spears. Bon appétit!

41. Stuffed Zucchini with Tofu and Cashews

4 Servings **50 minutes**

Ingredients

- 1 tablespoon olive oil
- 2 (12-ounce) packages firm tofu, drained and crumbled
- 2 garlic cloves, pressed
- 1/2 cup scallions, chopped
- 2 cups tomato puree
- 1/4 teaspoon turmeric
- 1/4 teaspoon chili powder
- Sea salt and cayenne pepper, to taste
- 4 zucchinis, cut into halves lengthwise and scoop out the insides
- 1 tablespoon nutritional yeast
- 2 ounces cashew nuts, lightly salted and choppedw

Directions

Heat the oil in a pan that is preheated over a moderate heat; now, cook the tofu, garlic, and scallions for 4 to 6 minutes.

Stir in 1 cup of the tomato puree and scooped zucchini flesh; add all seasonings and cook an additional 6 minutes, until the tofu is slightly browned.

Next, preheat your oven to 360 degrees F.

Divide the tofu mixture among the zucchini shells. Place the stuffed zucchini shells in a baking dish that is previously greased with a cooking spray. Pour in the remaining 1 cup of tomato puree.

Bake approximately 30 minutes. Sprinkle with nutritional yeast and cashew nuts; bake an additional 5 to 6 minutes. Enjoy!

Nutritional Information

148 Calories
10g Fat
4.8g Carbs
7.5g Protein
4g Fiber

4 Servings **15 minutes**

42. Broccoli Aloo Masala

Ingredients

- 3/4 pound broccoli, broken into florets
- 1/4 cup extra-virgin olive oil
- Seasoned salt and ground black pepper, to taste
- 1 garlic clove, smashed
- 1 tablespoon sesame paste
- 1 tablespoon fresh lime juice
- 1/2 teaspoon Garam Masala

Directions

Steam the broccoli for 7 minutes, until it is crisp-tender but still vibrant green. Pulse in your blender or a food processor until rice-like consistency is achieved.

Now, add the oil, salt, black paper, garlic, sesame paste, fresh lime juice and Garam Masala.

Blend until everything is well incorporated.

Drizzle with some extra olive oil and serve immediately. Otherwise, keep in your refrigerator until ready to serve.

Nutritional Information

100 Calories
8.2g Fat
4.7g Carbs
3.7g Protein
3.6g Fiber

43. Favourite Roasted Cabbage

6 Servings 45 minutes

Ingredients

- Nonstick cooking spray
- 2 pounds green cabbage, cut into wedges
- 1/4 cup olive oil
- Coarsely salt and freshly ground black pepper, to taste
- 1 teaspoon sesame seeds
- 2 tablespoons fresh chives, chopped

Nutritional Information

186 Calories
17g Fat
5.3g Carbs
2.1g Protein
3.3g Fiber

Directions

Begin by preheating your oven to 390 degrees F. Brush a rimmed baking sheet with a non-stick cooking spray.

Add the cabbage wedges to the baking sheet. Toss with olive oil, salt, black pepper and sesame seeds.

Roast for 40 to 45 minutes, until the cabbage is softened. Serve garnished with fresh chopped chives. Bon appétit!

4 Servings   15 minutes

44. Veggie Noodles with Hot Avocado Sauce

Ingredients

- 1/2 pound carrots
- 1/2 pound bell peppers
- 1 tablespoon olive oil
- 1 avocado, peeled and pitted
- 1 lemon, juiced and zested
- 2 tablespoons sesame oil
- 2 tablespoons cilantro, chopped
- 1 shallot, chopped
- 1 jalapeno pepper, deveined and minced
- Salt and black pepper, to taste

Nutritional Information

233 Calories
20.2g Fat;
6g Carbs
1.9g Protein
5g Fiber

Directions

Spiralize the carrots and bell peppers by using a spiralizer or a julienne peeler.

Heat the olive oil in a wok or a large nonstick skillet. Sauté the carrots and peppers in the hot olive oil for about 8 minutes.

Then, mix all remaining ingredients until creamy. Pour the avocado sauce over the noodles and serve immediately.

45. Cauliflower Rice Stuffed Peppers

4 Servings   40 minutes

Ingredients

- 1 small head cauliflower
- 4 bell peppers
- 1 ½ tablespoons oil
- 1 onion, chopped
- 1 garlic cloves, minced
- 1 teaspoon chipotle powder
- 1 teaspoon Berbere
- 2 ripe tomatoes, pureed
- Sea salt and pepper, to taste

Nutritional Information

77 Calories
4.8g Fat
5.4g Carbs
1.6g Protein
3.5g Fiber

Directions

To make the cauliflower rice, grate the cauliflower into the size of rice. Place on a kitchen towel to soak up any excess moisture.

Next, preheat your oven to 360 degrees F. Lightly grease a casserole dish.

Cut off the top of the bell peppers. Now, discard the seeds and core.

Roast the peppers in a parchment lined baking pan for 18 minutes until the skin is slightly browned.

In the meantime, heat the oil over medium-high heat. Sauté the onion and garlic until tender and fragrant.

Add the cauliflower rice, chipotle powder, and Berbere spice. Cook until the cauliflower rice is tender, about 6 minutes.

Divide the cauliflower mixture among the bell peppers. Place in the casserole dish.

Mix the tomatoes, salt, and pepper. Pour the tomato mixture over the peppers. Bake about 10 minutes, depending on desired tenderness. Serve immediately.

4 Servings   **20 minutes**

46. BBQ Asian Tofu with Tomato Sauce

Ingredients

- 10 ounces smoked tofu, pressed and drained
- 2 tablespoons olive oil
- 1 cup leeks, chopped
- 1 teaspoon garlic, minced
- 1/2 cup vegetable broth
- 1/2 teaspoon turmeric powder
- Sea salt and ground black pepper, to taste
- For the Sauce:
- 1/2 tablespoon olive oil
- 1 cup tomato sauce
- 2 tablespoons red wine
- 1 teaspoon fresh rosemary, chopped
- 1 teaspoon Asian chili garlic sauce

Directions

Pat dry the tofu and cut it into 1-inch cubes. Heat 2 tablespoons of the olive oil in a frying pan over a medium heat.

Then, fry the tofu cubes until they are slightly browned on all sides. Now, add the leeks, garlic, broth, turmeric powder, salt and pepper.

Cook until almost all liquid has evaporated.

Meanwhile, make the sauce. Heat 1/2 tablespoon of olive oil in a pan over a medium heat. Add the tomato sauce and cook until heated through.

Add the remaining ingredients and simmer over a medium-low heat approximately 10 minutes. Serve with prepared tofu cubes. Enjoy!

Nutritional Information

336 Calories
22.2g Fat
5.8g Carbs
27.6g Protein
4.7g Fiber

47. Parmesan-Crusted Vegetable Casserole

4 Servings   40 minutes

Ingredients

- 2 tablespoons olive oil
- 1 cup shallots, chopped
- 1 celery, chopped
- 2 carrots, grated
- 1/2 pound Brussels sprouts, quartered
- 1 cup roasted vegetable broth
- 1 teaspoon turmeric
- Sea salt and ground black pepper, to taste
- 1 teaspoon paprika powder
- 1/2 teaspoon liquid smoke
- 1 cup vegan parmesan
- 2 tablespoons fresh chives, roughly chopped

Directions

Start by preheating your oven to 360 degrees F. Brush a baking dish with olive oil.

In a heavy-bottomed skillet, heat the olive oil over a moderately high heat. Now, sweat the shallots until they are softened.

Add the celery, carrots and Brussels sprouts. Cook an additional 4 minutes or until just tender. Transfer the vegetable mixture to the baking dish.

Mix the roasted vegetable broth with the turmeric, salt, black pepper, paprika, and liquid smoke. Pour this mixture over the vegetables.

Top with vegan parmesan cheese and bake approximately 30 minutes. Serve garnished with fresh chives.

Nutritional Information

242 Calories
16.3g Fat
6.7g Carbs
16.3g Protein
4.1g Fiber

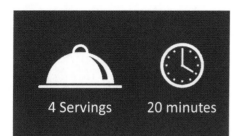

4 Servings   20 minutes

48. Saucy Fennel with Herb Tomato Sauce

Ingredients

- 2 tablespoons olive oil
- 1 garlic clove, crushed
- 1 fennel, thinly sliced
- 1/4 cup vegetable stock
- Sea salt and ground black pepper, to taste

For the Sauce:
- 2 tomatoes, halved
- 2 tablespoons extra-virgin olive oil
- 1/2 cup scallions, chopped
- 1 cloves garlic, minced
- 1 ancho chili, minced
- 1 bunch fresh basil, leaves picked
- 1 tablespoon fresh cilantro, roughly chopped
- Sat and pepper, to taste

Nutritional Information

135 Calories
13.6g Fat
3g Carbs
0.9g Protein
1.9g Fiber

Directions

Heat the olive oil in a pan over a moderately high heat. Sauté the garlic for 1 to 2 minutes or until aromatic.

Throw the slices of fennel into the pan; add the vegetable stock and continue to cook until the fennel has softened. Season with salt and black pepper to taste. Heat off.

Brush the tomato halves with extra-virgin olive oil.

Microwave for 15 minutes on HIGH; be sure to pour off any excess liquid.

Transfer the cooked tomatoes to a food processor; add the remaining ingredients for the sauce. Puree until your desired consistency is reached.

Serve with the sautéed fennel. Bon appétit!

49. Spicy Mushroom and Broccoli Melange

4 Servings   30 minutes

Ingredients

- Nonstick cooking spray
- 1 head broccoli, cut into florets
- 8 ounces cremini mushrooms, halved
- 2 garlic cloves, smashed
- 2 ripe tomatoes, pureed
- 1/4 cup vegan butter, melted
- 1 teaspoon hot paprika paste
- 1/4 teaspoon marjoram
- 1/2 teaspoon curry powder
- Coarse salt and black pepper, to taste

Directions

Begin by preheating your oven to 390 degrees F. Brush a baking dish with a nonstick cooking oil.

Next, arrange the broccoli and mushrooms in the baking dish. Scatter the smashed garlic around the vegetables. Add the pureed tomatoes.

Then, drizzle with the melted butter and add the hot paprika paste, marjoram, curry, salt, and black pepper.

Roast for 25 minutes, turning your baking dish once. Serve with a fresh salad of choice. Bon appétit!

Nutritional Information

113 Calories
 6.7g Fat
6.6g Carbs
5g Protein
5.9g Fiber

6 Servings   **30 minutes**

50. One-Skillet Tofu and Baby Artichokes

Ingredients

- 1 pound whole baby artichokes, cut off stems and tough outer leaves
- 2 tablespoons olive oil
- 2 blocks tofu, pressed and cubed
- 2 garlic cloves, minced
- 1 teaspoon Cajun spice mix
- 1 teaspoon deli mustard
- 1 bell pepper, chopped
- 1/4 cup vegetable broth
- Salt and pepper, to your liking

Directions

Cook the artichokes in a large saucepan of lightly salted water for 15 minutes or until they're tender; drain.

Heat the olive oil in a wok that is preheated over medium-high heat; add the tofu cubes and cook about 6 minutes, gently stirring.

Add the garlic and cook until aromatic or 30 seconds or so.

Add the remaining ingredients, including the reserved artichokes, and continue to cook 4 more minutes or until heated through. Serve warm on individual plates. Bon appétit!

Nutritional Information

138 Calories
8.9g Fat
6.8g Carbs
6.4g Protein
4.7g Fiber

51. Colorful Roasted Vegetables with Herbs

4 Servings   45 minutes

Ingredients

- 1 red bell pepper, deveined and sliced
- 1 green bell pepper, deveined and sliced
- 1 orange bell pepper, deveined and sliced
- 1/2 head of cauliflower, broken into large florets
- 2 zucchinis, cut into thick slices
- 2 medium-sized leeks, quartered
- 4 garlic cloves, halved
- 2 thyme sprigs, chopped
- 1 teaspoon dried sage, crushed
- 4 tablespoons olive oil
- 4 tablespoons tomato puree
- 1 teaspoon mixed whole peppercorns
- Sea salt and cayenne pepper, to taste

Directions

Preheat your oven to 425 degrees F. Sprits a rimmed baking sheet with a nonstick cooking spray.

Toss all of the above vegetables with the seasonings, oil and apple cider vinegar.

Roast about 40 minutes. Flip the vegetables halfway through the cooking time. Bon appétit!

Nutritional Information

165 Calories
14.3g Fat
5.6g Carbs
2.1g Protein
2.5g Fiber

SNACKS & APPETIZERS

52. Avocado Stuffed with Tomato and Mushrooms

8 Servings   10 minutes

Ingredients

- 4 avocados, pitted and halved
- 2 tablespoons olive oil
- 2 cups button mushrooms, chopped
- 1 onion, chopped
- 1 teaspoon garlic, crushed
- Salt and black pepper, to taste
- 1 teaspoon deli mustard
- 1 tomato, chopped

Directions

Scoop out about 2 teaspoons of avocado flesh from each half; reserve the scooped avocado flash.

Heat the oil in a sauté pan that is preheated over a moderately high flame. Now, cook the mushrooms, onion, and garlic until the mushrooms are tender and the onion is translucent.

Add the reserved avocado flash to the mushroom mixture and mix to combine. Now, add the salt, black pepper, mustard, and tomato.

Divide the mushroom mixture among the avocado halves and serve immediately.

Nutritional Information

245 Calories
23.2g Fat
8.2g Carbs
2.4g Protein
7.5g Fiber

53. Tofu-Kale Dip with Crudités

6 Servings   **25minutes**

Ingredients

- 2 cups kale
- 1 cup tofu, pressed, drained and crumbled
- 1/2 cup soy milk
- 2 teaspoons nutritional yeast
- 2 garlic cloves, minced
- 2 teaspoons olive oil
- 1 teaspoon sea salt
- 1/4 teaspoon ground black pepper, or more to taste
- 1/2 teaspoon paprika
- 1 teaspoon dried basil
- 1/2 teaspoon dried dill weed

Directions

Start by preheating your oven to 400 degrees F. Lightly oil a casserole dish with a nonstick cooking spray.

Now, parboil the kale leaves until it is just wilted.

Puree the remaining ingredients in your food processor or blender. Stir in the kale; stir until the mixture is homogeneous.

Bake approximately 13 minutes. Now, serve with a crudités platter. Bon appétit!

Nutritional Information

75 Calories
3g Fat
5g Carbs
2.9g Protein
1.2g Fiber

54. Italian-Style Stuffed Mushrooms

4 Servings   35 minutes

Ingredients

- 1/2 head cauliflower
- 1 pound medium-sized brown cremini mushrooms, cleaned and stems removed
- 2 tablespoons vegetable oil
- 1 onion, finely chopped
- 1 teaspoon garlic, minced
- 1 bell pepper, chopped
- 1 teaspoon Italian seasoning mix
- Salt and black pepper, to taste
- 1 cup vegan parmesan

Nutritional Information

206 Calories
13.4g Fat
5.6g Carbs
12.7g Protein
2.6g Fiber

Directions

Cook the cauliflower in a large pot of salted water until tender, about 6 minutes; cut into florets.

Then, pulse the cauliflower florets in your food processor until they resemble small rice-like granules.

Preheat an oven to 360 degrees F. Now, bake the mushroom caps for 8 to 12 minutes or until they are just tender.

Heat the oil in a heavy-bottomed skillet; sauté the onion, garlic and bell pepper until they have softened.

Add the Italian seasoning mix along with the salt and pepper; taste and adjust the seasonings. Fold in the cauliflower rice.

Next, divide the filling mixture among the mushroom caps. Top with vegan parmesan and bake 17 minutes longer. Serve warm.

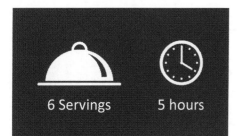

6 Servings   **5 hours**

55. Crispy Tomato Chips

Ingredients

- 1 ½ pounds tomatoes, sliced
- 1/4 cup extra-virgin olive oil
- 1 tablespoon Italian seasoning mix

For Vegan Parmesan:
- 1/2 cup pumpkin seeds
- 1 tablespoon nutritional yeast
- Salt and black pepper, to taste
- 1 teaspoon garlic powder

Directions

Drizzle the sliced tomatoes with olive oil.

Now, preheat your oven to 200 degrees F. Coat a baking pan with Silpat mat.

Pulse all the parmesan ingredients in your food processor until you reach a Parmesan cheese consistency.

Mix the parmesan with Italian seasoning mix. Then, toss the seasoned tomato slices with the parmesan mixture until they are well coated.

Arrange the tomato slices on the baking pan and bake for 5 hours. Store in an airtight container.

Nutritional Information

161 Calories
14g Fat;
6.2g Carbs
4.6g Protein
2g Fiber

56. Garlicky Spinach Chips with Avocado Dip

6 Servings   20 minutes

Ingredients

- 3 ripe avocados, pitted
- 2 teaspoons lime juice
- Salt and black pepper, to taste
- 2 garlic cloves, finely minced
- 2 tablespoons extra-virgin olive oil
- 1/2 teaspoon red pepper flakes
- For Spinach Chips:
- 2 cups baby spinach, washed and dried
- 1 tablespoon olive oil
- Sea salt and garlic powder, to taste

Directions

Mash the avocado pulp with a fork. Add the fresh lime juice, salt, pepper, garlic, and 2 tablespoons of olive oil.

Mix until everything is well incorporated. Transfer to a serving bowl and sprinkle with red pepper flakes.

Then, preheat your oven to 300 degrees F. Line a baking sheet with a Silpat mat.

Arrange the spinach leaves on the baking sheet; toss with 1 tablespoon of olive oil, salt, and garlic powder.

Bake for 8 to 12 minutes so the leaves have dried up. Serve with well-chilled avocado dip. Bon appétit!

Nutritional Information

269 Calories
26.7g Fat
7.4g Carbs
2.3g Protein
7g Fiber

8 Servings   10 minutes +
               chilling time

57. Authentic Mexican Guacamole

Ingredients

- 2 Haas avocados, peeled, pitted, and mashed
- 2 tablespoons fresh lime juice
- Sea salt and ground black pepper, to taste
- 1/2 teaspoon cumin, ground
- 1 yellow onion, chopped
- 2 tablespoons coriander leaves, chopped
- 1 cup fresh tomatoes, chopped
- 2 garlic cloves, minced
- 1 red chili, deseeded and finely chopped

Directions

In a bowl, thoroughly combine the avocados, lime juice, salt and black pepper.

Stir in the onion, cilantro, tomatoes, and garlic; sprinkle with paprika.

Keep in your refrigerator until ready to serve. Bon appétit!

Nutritional Information

112 Calories
9.9g Fat
6.5g Carbs
1.3g Protein
3.9g Fiber

58. Stuffed Avocado Boats

4 Servings   10 minutes

Ingredients

- 2 avocados, peeled and pitted
- 2 ounces pecans, ground
- 2 carrots, chopped
- 1 garlic clove
- 1 teaspoon lemon juice
- 1 tablespoon soy sauce
- Salt and freshly ground black pepper, to taste

Directions

In a mixing bowl, thoroughly combine the avocado pulp with the pecans, carrots, garlic, lemon juice, and soy sauce.

Season with salt and black pepper to taste. Divide the mixture among the avocado halves.

You can add some extra pecans for garnish. Bon appétit!

Nutritional Information

263 Calories
24.8g Fat
6.5g Carbs;
3.5g Protein
6g Fiber

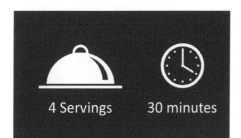

59. Stuffed Mushrooms with Walnuts

4 Servings   30 minutes

Ingredients

- 2 tablespoons sesame oil
- 1 cup onions, chopped
- 1 garlic clove, minced
- 1 pound white mushrooms, stems removed
- Salt and black pepper, to taste
- 1/4 cup raw walnuts, crushed
- 2 tablespoons cilantro, chopped

Nutritional Information

139 Calories
11.2g Fat
5.4g Carbs
4.8g Protein
3.6g Fiber

Directions

Begin by preheating an oven to 360 degrees F. Lightly grease a large baking sheet with a non-stick cooking spray.

Heat the sesame oil in a frying pan that is preheated over medium-high heat. Now, sauté the onions and garlic until aromatic.

Then, chop the mushroom stems and cook until they are tender. Heat off, season with salt and pepper; stir in the walnuts.

Stuff the mushroom caps with the walnut/mushroom mixture and arrange them on the prepared baking sheet.

Bake for 25 minutes and transfer to a wire rack to cool slightly. Garnish with fresh cilantro and serve. Bon appétit!

60. No Bake Fat Bombs

12 Servings **10 minutes**

Ingredients

- 2 cups ground almond flour
- 1/2 cup coconut oil
- 4 tablespoons erythritol
- 1/2 teaspoon pure vanilla extract
- 1/2 teaspoon pure coconut extract
- 1/4 teaspoon ground cinnamon
- 1/4 teaspoon kosher salt
- 2 tablespoons cocoa powder, unsweetened

Nutritional Information

173 Calories
17.2g Fat
4g Carbs
3.5g Protein
2.3g Fiber

Directions

Thoroughly combine all ingredients in a mixing bowl.

Shape the mixture into bite-sized balls; serve immediately or store in your refrigerator until ready to use. Bon appétit!

DESSERTS

61. Ultimate Peanut Butter Cookies

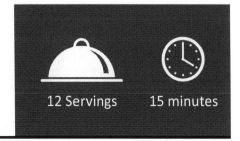

12 Servings   15 minutes

Ingredients

1 ¼ cups peanut butter

1 cup granulated monk fruit

2 tablespoons flaxseed meal

2 tablespoons ground chia seeds

Directions

Start by preheating your oven to 360 degrees F. Then, coat a baking pan with parchment paper.

In a mixing bowl, thoroughly combine all ingredients until everything is well incorporated.

Shape the mixture into bite-sized balls. Press each ball into a cookie shape using a fork.

Bake in the preheated oven for 9 minutes, or until lightly golden at the edges. Place your cookies on wire racks before serving. Enjoy!

Nutritional Information

143 Calories

9.3g Fat;

7.4g Carbs

6.8g Protein

2.4g Fiber

12 Servings **15 minutes**

62. Chocolate Almond Cookies

Ingredients

- 1 cup almond flour
- 1/2 cup almond butter
- 1/2 cup sesame butter
- 1/2 cup granulated Erythritol
- 2 tablespoons chia seeds, ground
- 1 teaspoon vanilla extract
- 1/4 teaspoon grated nutmeg
- 1/4 cup cocoa, unsweetened

Directions

Start by preheating your oven to 360 degrees F. Prepare a silicone baking sheet.

Then, combine all ingredients with a hand mixer.

Using a cookie scoop or your hands, form the dough into small balls. Arrange them on the prepared baking sheet.

Press lightly using a spoon. Bake in the pre-heated oven for about 10 minutes, or until lightly golden at the edges. Bon appétit!

Nutritional Information

178 Calories
15.4g Fat
6.4g Carbs
6.1g Protein
3.2g Fiber

63. Cinnamon Brownie Bars

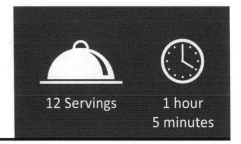

12 Servings

1 hour 5 minutes

Ingredients

- 1/2 cup almonds, ground
- 1/2 cup walnuts, ground
- 1 cup granulated monk fruit
- 1/3 cup cocoa powder, unsweetened
- 1 teaspoon ground cinnamon
- 1/2 teaspoon vanilla extract
- 2 tablespoons coconut oil
- A pinch of sea salt

Nutritional Information

71 Calories
6.7g Fat
2.9g Carbs
1.7g Protein
1.5g Fiber

Directions

Mix all ingredients until everything is well incorporated. Scrape the batter into a lightly greased baking sheet.

Let it sit in your freezer for 1 hour.

Cut into squares and serve well chilled. Enjoy!

5 Servings   **15 minutes**

64. Easy Raspberry Jam

Ingredients

- 1 cup raspberries, fresh or frozen
- 4 tablespoons chia seeds, ground
- 1/4 teaspoon ground cloves
- 1 teaspoon vanilla paste
- 1/3 cup water
- 1 teaspoon orange juice
- 1 teaspoon orange zest
- 2 tablespoons powdered monk fruit

Nutritional Information

71 Calories
3.6g Fat
7.3g Carbs
2.2g Protein
5.5g Fiber

Directions

Combine all ingredients in thr bowl of your food processor. Puree the mixture to the desired consistency.

Taste and adjust for sweetness.

Place your jam in a jar and store in the refrigerator.

65. Raspberry and Almond Swirl Cheesecake

8 Servings

3 hours
10 minutes

Ingredients

Crust:
- 1 cup blanched almond flour
- 1 tablespoon coconut oil
- 1/8 teaspoon grated nutmeg
- 1/4 teaspoon kosher salt
- 1/2 teaspoon liquid stevia
- Cheesecake:
- 1 cup blanched almonds, soaked in hot water for 2 hours
- 1/4 cup almond milk
- 1/2 cup coconut oil, melted
- 1 teaspoon vanilla paste
- 2 tablespoons fresh lime juice

Filling:
- 1 cup keto raspberry jam, preferably homemade

Nutritional Information

216 Calories
21.6g Fat
4.9g Carbs
2.9g Protein
2.5g Fiber

Directions

In your food processor, pulse together all ingredients for the crust. Press the almond crust into a small baking pan lined with parchment paper. Set aside.

Drain and rinse the soaked almonds; pulse your almonds in a food processor until a ball forms.

Stir in the remaining ingredients for the cheesecake and blend again until creamy and smooth.

Pour the mixture over the prepared crust and let it sit in your freezer for about 3 hours or until set.

Top your cheesecake with small spoonfuls of raspberry jam; use a toothpick to create swirl patterns on top of the cheesecake. Enjoy!

6 Servings

1 hour 10 minutes

66. Perfect Peppermint Fudge

Ingredients

- 1/2 cup coconut oil, melted
- 1/3 cup sugar-free chocolate chips, melted
- 1/4 cup hemp hearts, soaked overnight and rinsed
- 1 teaspoon peppermint extract
- 1/8 teaspoon kosher salt
- 1/8 teaspoon nutmeg, preferably freshly grated

Directions

Pulse all ingredients in your food processor until smooth and uniform.

Spoon the prepared mixture into a baking pan. Place you fudge in the refrigerator for 1 hour.

Allow your fudge to cool completely before cutting into 1-inch squares. Bon appétit!

Nutritional Information

191 Calories;
20.2g Fat
3.6g Carbs
1g Protein
0.2g Fiber

67. Chewy Chocolate and Peanut Butter Bars

8 Servings   25 minutes

Ingredients

- Base Layer:
- 1/2 cup peanut butter
- 2 tablespoons ground almonds
- 2 tablespoons granulated monk fruit

Top Layer:
- 1/4 cup peanut butter
- 1/4 cup sesame butter
- 2 tablespoons cocoa powder, unsweetened
- 1 tablespoon granulated monk fruit
- 2 tablespoons coconut flour

Directions

Mix all ingredients for the base layer in a bowl; in a separate bowl, mix the ingredients for the top layer. Mix to combine well.

Line a baking pan with parchment paper. Spread the base layer on the parchment paper; spread the top layer on it and transfer to the preheated oven.

Bake for 20 to 22 minutes at 350 degrees F. Place on wire racks before cutting and serving. Bon appétit!

Nutritional Information

237 Calories
19.9g Fat
7.3g Carbs
7.6g Protein
2.8g Fiber

68. Festive Butterscotch Blondies

12 Servings　　**25 minutes**

Ingredients

- 1 tablespoon flaxseed meal
- 4 tablespoons almond milk
- 1 cup almond butter
- 1/4 cup granulated monk fruit
- 1/4 teaspoon grated nutmeg
- 1 teaspoon vanilla extract
- 1 teaspoon baking powder
- A pinch of salt
- 1/2 cup vegan butterscotch chips

Nutritional Information

162 Calories
13.2g Fat;
6.2g Carbs
5.1g Protein
3g Fiber

Directions

Start by preheating your oven to 350 degrees F; now, line a baking dish with parchment paper and set aside.

In a mixing bowl, thoroughly combine the flaxseed meal, almond milk, almond butter, granulated monk fruit, nutmeg, vanilla, baking powder, and salt; mix until everything is well incorporated. Fold in the butterscotch chips.

Press the batter into the prepared baking dish; press it using a wide spatula or your hands.

Bake in the preheated oven for about 18 minutes or until it is lightly golden; transfer to a cooling rack before slicing and serving. Enjoy!

69. Blackberry Jam Sandwich Cookies

10 Servings

2 hours 40 minutes

Ingredients

Filling:
- 16 ounces fresh blackberries
- 1/4 cup granulated Swerve
- 1/8 teaspoon xanthan gum

Cookies:
- 3 cups unsweetened coconut, shredded
- 4 tablespoons monk fruit sweetener
- 1/3 cup coconut milk
- 1/2 teaspoon vanilla extract

Nutritional Information

119 Calories
9.8g Fat
7.2g Carbs
1.6g Protein
4.6g Fiber

Directions

Place the blackberries and granulated Swerve in your slow cooker. Cook for 2 hours 30 minutes on low heat.

Afterwards, stir in the xanthan gum to thicken the jam.

Meanwhile, pulse all ingredients for the cookies until everything is well combined. Now, roll the batter until 1/4-thick.

Place on a parchment paper-lined baking sheet and chill until firm or at least 1 hour. Using a 2-inch fluted round cutter, cut out the cookies.

Spread half the cookies with 1/2 teaspoon of jam each; assemble the cookie sandwiches with the rest of the cookies. Bon appétit!

8 Servings   40 minutes

70. Coconut Carrot Cake Squares

Ingredients

Carrot Cake Base:
- 1 cup coconut flour
- 1 cup water
- 4 tablespoons applesauce, unsweetened
- 1/4 teaspoon ground cloves
- 1 teaspoon vanilla extract
- 1 teaspoon ground cinnamon
- 1/4 cup granulated monk fruit
- 1 large carrot, shredded

Topping:
- 1/4 cup shredded coconut

Nutritional Information

53 Calories
4.2g Fat
3.9g Carbs
0.7g Protein
1.6g Fiber

Directions

Mix all ingredients for the carrot cake base until well combined.

Press the mixture into a parchment-lined baking pan. Place in your refrigerator for 30 minutes.

Scatter the shredded coconut over the top and cut into squares. Enjoy!

71. The Best Avocado Cupcakes Ever

12 Servings   30 minutes

Ingredients

- 1/2 cup ripe avocado, mashed
- 1/3 cup coconut oil
- 1 cup hot water
- 1 tablespoon instant coffee
- 1 cup coconut flour
- 1 cup cocoa powder, unsweetened
- 8 ounces erythritol
- 1 teaspoon baking soda
- 1/2 teaspoon vanilla extract
- 1/4 teaspoon ground cardamom
- 1/4 teaspoon kosher salt

Directions

Start by preheating your oven to 355 degrees F. Prepare the cupcake molds and set aside.

In a mixing bowl, thoroughly combine the avocado with the coconut oil. Dissolve the instant coffee in hot water and stir into the avocado mixture.

Stir in the other ingredients. Divide the batter between the cupcake molds. Bake in the pre-heated oven for 20 to 25 minutes.

Transfer to a wire rack to cool completely. Bon appétit!

Nutritional Information

107 Calories
10.5g Fat;
6.2g Carbs
1.7g Protein
3.4g Fiber

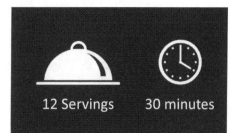

12 Servings **30 minutes**

72. Key Lime Mini Cheesecakes

Ingredients

Crust:
- 1 cup almond meal
- 4 tablespoons coconut oil
- A pinch of salt
- A pinch of freshly grated nutmeg

Cheesecake:
- 1 cup cashews, soaked in hot water for 2 hours
- 1/4 cup almond milk
- 1/2 cup coconut oil, melted
- 1 tablespoon fresh key lime juice
- 1 teaspoon key lime zest, grated
- 1 teaspoon vanilla paste

Nutritional Information

167 Calories
17.5g Fat
2.9g Carbs
1.7g Protein
0.3g Fiber

Directions

Line a muffin tin with cupcake liners and set aside.

In your food processor, pulse together all ingredients for the crust. Press the crust into the bottom of a muffin tin.

Bake the crusts at 350 degrees F for about 5 minutes or until it is slightly brown and crispy.

Drain and rinse the soaked cashews; pulse in a food processor until a ball forms. Stir in the remaining ingredients for the cheesecake and blend until creamy.

Pour the mixture over the prepared crust. Let them cool in the refrigerator overnight. Bon appétit!

73. Home-Style Chocolate Bar

4 Servings   30 minutes

Ingredients

- 6 tablespoons coconut oil
- 2 ounces sugar-free unsweetened baker's chocolate
- 2 tablespoons tofu, pureed
- 4 tablespoons powdered erythritol
- 1/2 teaspoon vanilla extract
- 1/4 teaspoon grated nutmeg
- 1/4 teaspoon ground cloves
- 1/8 teaspoon coarse sea salt

Directions

Microwave the coconut oil and chocolate and stir well. Stir in the tofu and powdered erythritol.

Add the remaining ingredients and stir until everything is well combined. Pour the chocolate mixture into a chocolate mold.

Freeze for 1 to 2 hours and serve!

Nutritional Information

190 Calories
20.8g Fat
3.3g Carbs
0.7g Protein;
0.4g Fiber

4 Servings

10 minutes + chilling time

74. Chocolate Avocado Pudding

Ingredients

- 1 ½ cups canned full-fat coconut milk
- 1/2 cup cacao powder, unsweetened
- 1 teaspoon pure vanilla extract
- 1/4 teaspoon grated nutmeg
- 1/2 teaspoon ground cinnamon
- 1/8 teaspoon kosher salt
- 1 avocado, peeled, pitted and mashed
- 1/2 cup powdered monk fruit

Directions

Heat the coconut milk and cacao powder in a saucepan over low heat; stir to combine well.

Remove from the heat and cool slightly. Transfer the mixture to a blender and stir in the remaining ingredients.

Blend until creamy and uniform. Place in your refrigerator for 2 to 3 hours. Serve well-chilled!

Nutritional Information

226 Calories
21.1g Fat
7.7g Carbs
4.7g Protein
5g Fiber

75. Old-Fashioned Walnut Cookies

8 Servings

10 minutes + chilling time

Ingredients

- 1/2 cup almond meal
- 1/2 cup coconut flour
- 2 cups no-sugar dairy-free chocolate spread
- 1/2 cup monk fruit
- 1/2 teaspoon vanilla extract
- 1/2 teaspoon ground cinnamon
- 1/4 teaspoon ground cardamom
- 2 tablespoon almond milk
- 1 cup walnuts, finely chopped

Directions

Coat a cookie sheet with parchment paper; set aside.

Thoroughly combine all ingredients, except for the walnuts, in a mixing bowl. Roll the mixture into bite-sized balls.

Arrange these balls on the prepared cookie sheet.

In a shallow dish, place the walnuts. Cover the prepared cookies with the chopped walnuts and press them into a cookie shape; place in your refrigerator until firm. Bon appétit!

Nutritional Information

200 Calories
18g Fat
7.8g Carbs
6.6g Protein
4.9g Fiber

Made in the USA
Columbia, SC
02 November 2019

82582293R00054